READING BARTH
WITH CHARITY

READING BARTH WITH CHARITY

A Hermeneutical Proposal

GEORGE HUNSINGER

B
BakerAcademic
a division of Baker Publishing Group
Grand Rapids, Michigan

Published by Baker Academic
a division of Baker Publishing Group
P.O. Box 6287, Grand Rapids, MI 49516-6287
www.bakeracademic.com

Printed in the United States of America

Library of Congress Cataloging-in-Publication Data is on file at the Library of Congress, Washington, DC.

ISBN 978-0-8010-9531-3

15 16 17 18 19 20 21   7 6 5 4 3 2 1

Contents

ACKNOWLEDGMENTS

I would like to thank the members of the Yale-Washington Theology Group for their incisive and helpful comments. I also profited especially from the suggestions of Khaled Anatolios, Matthew Baker, James J. Buckley, Paul L. Gavrilyuk, Matthew Levering, and William Werpehowski. Paul D. Molnar and my dear wife, Deborah van Deusen Hunsinger, read through the entire manuscript with keen eyes, offering invaluable advice in helping me to improve the text. I could not have asked for better editors than David Nelson and Christina Jasko, who were encouraging throughout. Responsibility for the final product is of course my own.

Abbreviations

CD	Karl Barth, *Church Dogmatics*
De Trin.	Hilary of Poitiers, *De Trinitate*
Inst.	John Calvin, *Institutes of the Christian Religion*
KD	Karl Barth, *Kirchliche Dogmatik*
Or.	Gregory Nazianzen, *Orations*
Or. Cat.	Gregory of Nyssa, *Catechetical Oration*
rev.	revised translation
S. theol.	Thomas Aquinas, *Summa Theologica*
sec.	section

Introduction

Recently the world of Barth studies has been rocked by an internal debate. As is familiar by now, certain scholars, whom I will call "revisionists," contend that for Barth, God's pretemporal decision of election in Christ is the ground of God's trinitarian identity. In effect what this means is this: No election, no Trinity. "Traditionalist" interpreters like myself, on the other hand, reject this view as misguided. The evidence in Barth, they believe, points very much in the opposite direction: No Trinity, no election. For Barth, according to the traditionalists, God's pretemporal decision of election presupposes God's prior reality as the Trinity. God's trinitarian identity in no way depends on election.

I embark on this present study because I am puzzled by how the revisionists have responded to their critics. I had expected that they would do more to come to terms with the considerable body of counterevidence. I had imagined that important texts disconfirming their position would be more fully addressed. For example, in *Church Dogmatics*, volume II, part 2—the volume that is said to shift decisively in the revisionist direction—Barth states that Jesus Christ's identity as God's Son "of course does not rest on election."[1]

1. *Beruht freilich nicht auf Erwählung*. Karl Barth, *Church Dogmatics*, vol. II, part 2 (Edinburgh: T&T Clark, 1942), 107; *Kirchliche Dogmatik*, vol. II, part 2 (Zurich: Theologischer Verlag Zurich, 1942), 114. Hereafter references to volumes

As telling as it is, this statement is far from isolated. Many related passages can be found throughout the *Church Dogmatics*. One finds them not only prior to Barth's supposed change but also within II/2 itself, and then afterward, all the way through to the last volumes of his dogmatics. I have wondered why this body of material doesn't give the revisionists more pause. Although they know about it, they proceed as if it can be safely placed to one side without damaging their case. This is the procedure that has puzzled me. I propose to explore what may lie behind it.

The Principle of Charity

In recent analytical philosophy, an appeal is commonly made to "the principle of charity." It is designed to guide the interpretation of texts, especially difficult or ambiguous texts. Although there is no single authoritative definition, the principle of charity is widely taken for granted in the practice of contemporary philosophy. Here is a summary of what is involved.[2]

- The principle of charity seeks to understand a point of view in its strongest form before subjecting it to criticism.

  A suspension of one's own beliefs may be required in order to attain a sympathetic understanding.
- One assumes for the moment that the ideas under consideration, regardless of how difficult they may seem, are both true and internally coherent.

  The emphasis falls on seeking to understand the texts as they stand rather than on picking out difficulties or contradictions.
- If apparent contradictions are found, an active attempt is made to resolve them.

---

of Barth's *Church Dogmatics* (1936–69) will be cited in the text according to convention along the lines of II/2.

2. See "Donald Davidson: Principle of Charity," *Stanford Encyclopedia of Philosophy*, http://plato.stanford.edu/entries/davidson/; "The Principle of Charity," *Lander University Website*, http://philosophy.lander.edu/oriental/charity.html.

Donald Davidson has suggested, for example, that the principle of charity means attempting to maximize sense and optimize agreement when it comes to doubts about the inner coherence or factual veracity of the viewpoint under consideration.[3]

- If it is possible to resolve apparent contradictions (or ambiguities) through a sympathetic interpretation, a presumption exists in favor of that interpretation.

  A presumption exists by the same token against any interpretation that resorts to the charge of inconsistency without attempting to resolve apparent contradictions.

- Only if no successful interpretation can be found is one entitled to conclude that a viewpoint is inconsistent or false.

  Critique is always possible but only after an adequate effort has been made for an interpretation that does not call a viewpoint's truth or coherence into question precipitously.

- The attempt to maximize intelligibility through the resolution of apparent contradictions is related to a corollary, which is called "the principle of humanity."

  As Daniel Dennett explains, one should attribute to the person whose views one is considering "the propositional attitudes one supposes one would have oneself in those circumstances."[4]

The principle of charity gives us a set of criteria by which to assess the revisionist position.

- Does it seek to understand Barth's theology in its strongest form before subjecting it to fundamental criticism?
- Has it truly sought to understand Barth before picking out supposed difficulties or contradictions?
- If apparent contradictions are discerned (as they are), has an active attempt been made to resolve them in Barth's favor?

3. Donald Davidson, "Three Varieties of Knowledge," in *Subjective, Intersubjective, Objective: Philosophical Essays* (New York: Oxford University Press, 2001), 205–20.

4. Daniel C. Dennett, "Mid-term Examination," in *The Intentional Stance* (Boston: MIT Press, 1987), 339–50; on 343.

- If no such attempt has been made (as it has not), does not a certain presumption exist against this interpretation?
- Finally, do the revisionists honor the principle of humanity, or do they seem to adopt an attitude of condescension toward the writer whose views they are considering?
- In short, are the revisionists entitled to their key claim that Barth's views on election and the Trinity, when taken as a whole, are "inconsistent"?

These are my preliminary questions for the revisionists.

Evangelical Calvinism and Rationalistic Calvinism

Before pursuing this line of inquiry, a second line will also be opened up. In the writings of Thomas F. Torrance, a distinction is made between "evangelical Calvinism" and "rationalistic Calvinism."[5] Although these terms point mainly to differences in content, it is a divergence in the mode of reasoning that interests me. Despite the ways in which their contents may overlap, rationalistic Calvinism departs from evangelical Calvinism by its *modus operandi*.

Evangelical Calvinism, as explained by Torrance, was a minority position in Anglo-Saxon Calvinism, although he believed it to be closer to Calvin himself. Torrance associated it with John Knox and the 1560 Scots Confession, to which he might have added the Heidelberg Catechism. By comparison with its more influential cousin, the idiom of evangelical Calvinism was more biblical and less scholastic. It retained a more open-textured structure as opposed to a taste for sharp distinctions and scholastic rigor. It believed that theological statements pointed away from themselves to the truth about God, which by its nature could not be contained in finite forms of speech

5. See Thomas F. Torrance, *Scottish Theology: From John Knox to John McLeod Campbell* (Edinburgh: T&T Clark, 1996), 129–33. (Further references, which are scattered throughout the book, can be found by using the index.) See also Torrance, "From John Knox to John McLeod Campbell: A Reading of Scottish Theology," in *Disruption to Diversity: Edinburgh Divinity 1846–1996*, ed. David F. Wright and Gary D. Badcock (Edinburgh: T&T Clark, 1996), 1–28.

and thought, but also that without theological statements, such truth could not be mediated. It judged, according to Torrance, that the filial was prior to the legal, that the personal was prior to the propositional, that the inductive took precedence over the deductive, and that spiritual insight placed constraints on logical reasoning.

The priorities of rationalistic Calvinism were more or less the reverse. Rationalistic Calvinism, for Torrance, was associated with Theodore Beza, the Westminster standards (1646–48), and the Synod of Dordt (1618–19). It was known for such extreme outcomes as limited atonement, a debate between "supralapsarianism" and "infralapsarianism," and a legalistic construal of "covenant" that tended toward synergism. These unfortunate ideas reflected a certain mode of reasoning. The legal was prior to the filial, the deductive to the inductive, and the propositional to the personal. There was a general tendency to draw logical conclusions from abstract propositions and to arrange the results in water-tight systems. As Torrance saw it, this type of Calvinism predominated from roughly 1650 to 1950 in the Anglo-Saxon world, especially in Scotland and the United States.

A statement by Hilary of Poitiers, the fourth-century doctor of the church, can help to focus this contrast. He wrote, "*Non sermoni res, sed rei sermo subjectus est*" (*De Trin.* 4.14). Loosely translated, this might read, "It is not the concepts that dictate the subject matter, but the subject matter that dictates the concepts." Rationalistic Calvinism tended to reason from the concepts to the subject matter. It argued that certain beliefs must be true because they followed logically from certain abstract propositions. In that sense the subject matter was dictated by the concepts. Evangelical Calvinism, on the other hand, tended to do the opposite by reasoning from the subject matter to the concepts. It refrained from what it regarded as a false application of logical rigor because of constraints imposed by the subject matter itself. In that sense the concepts were dictated by the subject matter, even if they had to be left in tension. Rationalistic Calvinists, for example, argued rigorously from double predestination to limited atonement, whereas at least some evangelical Calvinists resisted those conclusions. Instead they gave priority to scriptural affirmations that Christ died for all, even though they could not resolve all the remaining perplexities. The difference between the two forms of Calvinism was, to a significant degree, the difference between deductive and inductive reasoning.[6]

When we turn to the revisionist proposal about election and the Trinity, the above analysis seems relevant. The reasoning of the Barthian revisionists seems closer to rationalistic Calvinism than to evangelical Calvinism. I am not thinking of doctrines like limited atonement, supralapsarianism, or of viewing God's covenant as though it were a contract. Rather, I mean the underlying assumptions that led to such outcomes. What seems to be at stake in both cases—that is, in both rationalistic Calvinism and Barthian revisionism—is a certain style of reasoning. It gravitates toward propositions taken out of context and draws logical deductions from them. Complex dialectical positions are reduced to a set of relatively simple assertions from which erroneous conclusions can be drawn.

I am convinced that the Barthian-revisionist viewpoint rests, to a large degree, on a series of unwarranted inferences. At the same time it also fails to honor the principle of charity. These methodological failings help to explain revisionism's tendency to disregard the evidence against it. At the most general level, that is the narrative I set out to relate.

6. An interesting chart drafted by B. B. Warfield unwittingly reveals how much of an outlier rationalistic Calvinism has been within the context of world Christianity. See Warfield, *The Plan of Salvation* (Grand Rapids: Eerdmans, 1980), 30.

1

Grace and Being
The Charter Document

The elements of the revisionist argument call for careful attention. The place to begin is the essay by Bruce McCormack titled "Grace and Being: The Role of God's Gracious Election in Karl Barth's Theological Ontology."[1] Although revisionism has evolved to some extent since this essay was written, "Grace and Being" still stands out, in effect, as the manifesto of the revisionist movement.[2]

Ontology

Let's begin with the idea of "ontology." It is assumed without argument that Karl Barth operates with an ontology. We have recently witnessed a veritable explosion of writings connecting "ontology"

1. Bruce McCormack, "Grace and Being: The Role of God's Gracious Election in Karl Barth's Theological Ontology," in *The Cambridge Companion to Karl Barth* (Cambridge: Cambridge University Press, 2000), 92–110.

2. Among the names associated with the new Barth-revisionism are Paul T. Nimmo, Paul Dafydd Jones, Matthias Gockel, and others. I take up their writings in due course.

with Barth. He is said to have a "theological ontology," as in the title of this essay, but elsewhere in contemporary discussion we find him operating with a moral ontology, an eschatological ontology, a soteriological ontology, a social ontology, and—most highly prized of all—an "actualistic ontology." Of ontologies in Barth, it would seem, there is no end. But what does all this "ontology talk" really mean? I'm sure it would have astonished Barth, and I'm not sure it would have pleased him.

The word *ontology* is ambiguous, having more than one possible meaning. Roughly speaking, there is a proper sense and an extended sense. In the philosophical or proper sense, "ontology" refers to the study of being. It is a branch of metaphysics that deals comprehensively with the nature of being and of beings. In the extended sense, on the other hand, the term refers to something looser. It signifies only a field of inquiry pertaining to the material covered and the sorts of things and relations one finds in it—to a general area of action, inquiry, or interest. It is descriptive with no claims of being systematic or explanatory. Following the literary conventions of the philosopher Charles Taylor, I will call the proper sense "ontology_1" and the extended sense "ontology_2."[3]

It seems that the revisionists do not take sufficient pains to distinguish ontology_1 from ontology_2. Too often they seem to trade on the ambiguity, appearing to speak of ontology_2 while slipping into ontology_1. The slippage can have unfortunate consequences, as will be seen. But first we need to recall that while occasionally allowing for ontology_2, Barth always polemicized against ontology_1.

An early indication of Barth's attitude can be found in his letter to Rudolf Bultmann from June 12, 1928.[4] "I have come to abhor profoundly," Barth wrote, "the spectacle of theology constantly trying above all to adjust to the philosophy of the age, thereby neglecting its own theme" (41). This was said in response to Bultmann's urging him to leave behind outmoded Platonic and Aristotelian thought forms in favor of Heidegger's ontology. Barth continued,

3. In *A Secular Age* (Cambridge, MA: Belknap Press of Harvard University Press, 2007), Taylor regularly disambiguates terms by resorting to the use of subscripts.

4. See *Karl Barth/Rudolf Bultmann, Letters 1922–1966*, ed. Bernd Jaspert (Grand Rapids: Eerdmans, 1981), 40–42.

> The Platonism and Aristotelianism of the orthodox was not a hindrance to my . . . perceiving what was at issue and therefore to adopting the older terminology into my own vocabulary without identifying myself with the underlying philosophy. (41)
>
> With reference to matters that I saw to be at issue in the Bible and the history of dogma, I have reached out on the right hand and the left for terms or concepts that I found to be most appropriate . . . because my hands were already full trying to *say* something very specific. (41)
>
> My own concern is to hear at any rate the voice of the church and the Bible, and to let this voice be heard, even if in so doing, for want of anything better, I have to think somewhat in Aristotelian terms. (42)

By the late 1920s Barth's lifelong approach to various philosophies was already in place. It was eclectic, unsystematic, and ad hoc. He had no desire to adopt a thoroughgoing Heideggerian framework, which was, of course, a quintessential version of ontology$_1$.

For Barth ontology$_1$ represented a danger for dogmatic theology. No ontology ought to become a systematic framework within which theology was constrained to operate. For example, if an ontological system were set up that embraced both God and the creature, an impossible situation would arise where the creature posed "conditions for God" (II/1, 583). Barth argued that philosophical criteria, such as ontology$_1$ would introduce, have no direct role to play in dogmatic reflection. Those who believe otherwise, he suggested, should be quietly asked to desist from doing theological work, where they "can only cause confusion with these and other standards" (I/1, 285).

There can be, Barth wrote, no "ontology of the created totality. . . . The Word of God does not contain any ontology of heaven and earth themselves" (III/2, 6). Dogmatic theology should never hold fast to any comprehensive ontology "as if it were uniquely true and biblical and orthodox" (III/2, 7). "Any attempt at an independent [or explanatory] ontology . . . would at once estrange us" from the proper knowledge of God (III/3, 442). Christology in particular must avoid taking on "the appearance of an ontology and dramatics arbitrarily constructed from Scripture and tradition" (IV/1, 757). The event of the incarnation "cannot . . . be perceived or understood or deduced from any ontology which embraces God himself and the world, God himself and humankind, or from any higher standpoint whatever" (IV/2, 41, rev.).

As long as such stipulations are in place, the looser sense of ontology$_2$ is acceptable. Barth could describe Christian discipleship, for example, as "not so much a matter of morals as ontology" when it came to the saying that no disciple was above his or her master (Matt. 10:24). Here "ontology" is a matter of pointing to the proper order and status of particulars in a limited case.

To sum up: the important thing to see is that Barth's approach to ontology$_1$ was both negative and positive. Negatively, he always rejected it as a controlling system, while positively, his approach was eclectic. Ontology$_1$ could be raided for concepts to be used in an ad hoc and nonsystematic way, but no more. As a consequence, Barth would have harbored no intention to construct a thoroughly actualistic concept of God's being if that meant God's being was merely a consequence of God's actions, as required by prior ontological commitments. His emphasis was always on the a posteriori nature of theological reflection as based on revelation. A dogmatic theology that respected God as Wholly Other, and so as incommensurable with the world, precluded any kind of comprehensive ontological agenda.

Moreover, no ontology—in the sense of ontology$_1$—could be allowed to bracket together the creature and the Creator. The doctrine of God could not be absorbed into a doctrine of being—not even an actualistic doctrine of being. As Eberhard Jüngel has written, "Barth's *Dogmatics* makes ontological statements all the way through. But this dogmatics is not an ontology; at least not in the sense of a doctrine of being drawn up on the basis of a general ontological conception within which the being of God (as highest being, being-itself, etc.) would be treated in its place."[5]

This means, I believe, that Barth would have been averse to constructing a "postmetaphysical" theology. He would have opposed it for theological reasons. It would have carried a danger he always sought to avoid, namely, that of setting up a conceptual scheme in which God was conditioned by the world. Under no circumstances did he

5. Eberhard Jüngel, *God's Being Is in Becoming* (Edinburgh: T&T Clark, 2001), 76.

want that to happen. Whether revisionist Barthianism can avoid this outcome remains to be seen.

According to Professor McCormack, Barth's doctrine of election involves an implied ontology (107). This ontology is said to arise because for Barth the death of Christ is an event in the divine life (98). Whether to adopt some sort of ontology is not in question. The only choice is between an "actualistic ontology" and an "essentialist ontology" (98). "None of the above" is not an option.

For the revisionists, anyone who demurs from adopting an "actualistic ontology" is automatically saddled with an "essentialist ontology." No provision is made that this might be a Hobson's choice. By the same token, anyone who rejects the revisionists' "actualistic ontology" is ipso facto entangled in "classical metaphysics." If "classical metaphysics" (a term never defined) is actually a code word for traditional Catholicism and Eastern Orthodoxy, "actualistic ontology" might in turn be a cryptogram for some sort of hyper-Protestantism.[6]

The possibility that dogmatic theology might be actualistic in some ways while embracing classical metaphysics in other ways—which is what I think Barth actually does—is of course ruled out. The only alternative is to be either "actualistic" or "essentialist," with no gradations between. Barth's "actualistic ontology" supposedly committed him to purging all elements of "classical metaphysics" from his theology.[7]

Not much content is ascribed to Barth's "actualistic ontology" in the "Grace and Being" essay. That will come later. But we do learn at least two things about it. First, it functions to describe the being of God. It indicates that from all eternity God's being "is determined, *defined*, by what he reveals himself to be in Jesus Christ; viz., a God of love and mercy towards the whole human race" (97–98, italics added). Except for the slippery word *defined*, which we will come back to momentarily (as if the words *determined* and *defined* mean

6. By "hyper-Protestantism" I mean the idea that Protestantism must define its doctrine of God, at important points, in antithesis to traditional Catholicism and Eastern Orthodoxy (i.e., to figures like Thomas Aquinas and Gregory of Nazianzus).

7. Cf. Bruce L. McCormack: "I continue to believe that it was Barth's intention throughout all the phases of his development to elaborate a postmetaphysical understanding of God." McCormack, *Orthodox and Modern: Studies in the Theology of Karl Barth* (Grand Rapids: Baker Academic, 2008), 264. No statement of this intention can be found in Barth's writings.

the same thing), one does not need anything like an ontology to say this—certainly not in the sense of ontology$_1$. It would be more accurate to say that for Barth God reveals himself as a God of love and mercy toward the human race, that he is already a God of love antecedently in himself, and that in his pretemporal act of election God determines himself *also*—the word *also* is important here—to be a God of love and mercy for the world.

According to revisionism's "actualistic ontology," the act by which God's being is *constituted* is not first of all trinitarian. It is not the primordial act by which God is who he is, as Father, Son, and Holy Spirit to all eternity. It seems that there can be no such thing as this primordial trinitarian act. If God is really going to be a God who "acts," the divine activity must occur first *in relation to the world*. No other possibility can be entertained.

God's decision of pretemporal election is of course an action in relation to the world. Election is said to mean that "what God is essentially is itself *constituted* by an eternal act of Self-determination for becoming incarnate in time—in which case eternal divine action would ground divine essence" (96–97, italics added). This electing act in relation to the world is "*constitutive* of the divine essence" (a momentous claim; 96, italics original). God has no being in and of himself that is not "constituted" by God's relationship to the world through election. God has no perfect and determinate being in eternity prior to the decision of election.[8]

Professor McCormack's way of stating this more positively is to say that in the pretemporal decision of election, God "*gives himself being*" (e.g., 104, italics added). I do not find this to be a clear idea, but in any case it is puzzling. Even in the traditional view that the Father begets the Son eternally, so that the eternal being (*ousia*) of God just is the Father begetting the Son (as we find for example in Athanasius), no one would ever have thought to claim that God is thereby *giving*

8. Perhaps the first sign of this claim was worded as follows: "It is not simply that the being of God is made known to human beings in revelation; it is rather that the being of God is itself established in the act of revelation. God's being is a 'being in act.'" McCormack, *Karl Barth's Critically Realistic Dialectical Theology* (Oxford: Clarendon, 1995), 461. From a traditionalist standpoint, this is the root error of revisionism.

himself being. Would he be doing so *ex nihilo*? How does one give oneself something that one does not have, even if one is God?

Professor McCormack's statement means that he has to explain who (or what) this beingless "God" is prior to election and the Trinity, something I think that he has never successfully done. The idea of a God who gives himself being—which in effect posits a "God beyond God" (i.e., an initial "God" prior to election and the Trinity)—seems to result from the inner logic of revisionism's "actualistic ontology" as applied to election.

The idea of a perfect, determinate triune being prior to the decision of election—in other words, the traditional doctrine—is dismissed as something "abstract" (100) and "speculative" (92, 95, and *passim*).[9] If so, then it is not only the traditionalists who are in error but also Barth himself (and the whole ecumenical tradition). Prior to the volume on election (II/2) Barth embraced such a supposedly "essentialist" view, and even afterward he never entirely abandoned it, as the revisionists will sometimes admit. That is why they have rallied. They have appointed themselves to help Barth out, carrying through the "postmetaphysical" project that he so promisingly began but for some reason failed to fulfill. The revisionists will do it for him.

Second, in revisionism's "actualistic ontology," the pretemporal decision of election is not only thought to *define* the divine being. It also has an *explanatory* function. "How is it possible," we are asked, "for God to *become*, to enter fully into time as One who is subjected to the limitations of human life in this world, without undergoing any *essential* (i.e., ontological) change?" (96, italics original). In other words, how is it possible for God to become human in the incarnation without ceasing to be God? This is of course a very old question. Barth's standard answer—in line with the main ecumenical tradition at least since Athanasius and Cyril—is twofold.

First, Barth appeals to God's sovereign freedom. If God has actually done it, then it is possible for God to do it—by virtue of his freedom. If God has become human in Christ, for example, by entering fully into time without ceasing to be God, then the condition for

9. Barth never used the terms "abstract" and "speculative" in this way, as we will see momentarily.

this possibility—the necessary and sufficient condition—is found in his sovereign freedom and nowhere else. For Barth the incarnation neither has nor requires any other "explanation," and certainly not one that might require an "ontology," whether actualistic or not.[10]

The second aspect of Barth's standard answer is his doctrine of divine antecedence.[11] Everything that God does in time finds its antecedent ground in eternity. If God is loving toward the world, that is possible because God is already eternally loving in himself. If God relates to the world in freedom, that is possible because God is already free in himself to all eternity. If God reveals himself in history to be the Father, the Son, and the Holy Spirit, that is possible because God is already trinitarian in himself. And so on.[12]

The necessary and sufficient condition for the possibility of all God's ways and works toward the world is always located in God's antecedent being as the eternal Trinity. In other words, it is located in the triune God as the One who loves in freedom in and of himself. In abandoning the idea of the Trinity as subsisting prior to election, the revisionists abandon Barth's signature doctrine of antecedence. They replace it instead with their "actualistic ontology." In effect this means that Barth's doctrine of antecedence is replaced by a doctrine of subsequence. What God is eternally in himself is subsequent to what he determines himself to be relative to the world.

A question may be posed here for the revisionists. Which is really "abstract" and "speculative"—Barth's doctrine of antecedence or the resort to explanation by means of an actualistic ontology? For Barth something counted as "abstract" if it proceeded without basic reference to God's concrete activity. For him the antecedent Trinity was not something abstract; it was indeed the *ens concretissimum*. Nothing could be more concrete than the primordial act in which the eternal God enjoys his being in love and freedom as the Father, the Son, and the Holy Spirit. Barth did not limit his idea of divine

10. Statements about such core mysteries as God becoming human in the incarnation without ceasing to be God are "statements concerning the free activity of God" (I/1, 9).

11. I use the word *doctrine* here only as a matter of convenience. I do not mean to suggest that Barth has anything like a formal "doctrine of antecedence."

12. "God's love is in no way coincident with his being for us. He is the One who loves in himself quite apart from his relation to the existence of another" (II/1, 347–48).

activity to God's relations with the world. Only because the triune God was already active in himself could he also be active in the world.

For Barth something was "speculative," furthermore, if it proceeded without proper reference to God's historical self-revelation in Christ. For him the eternal Trinity was not a speculative idea, because the truth of God's self-revelation in time depended on its being true for God in eternity. Our knowledge of the Holy Trinity is true because it participates in the truth of the eternal God's own self-knowledge. It receives a share in the truth whereby the Father knows the Son, and the Son the Father, in the unity of the Holy Spirit, to all eternity. Far from being speculative, the idea of the eternal Trinity is the ground of all revealed truth (II/1, 16, 49, 51, 343–46, etc.).

For the revisionists, on the other hand, something is "abstract" and "speculative" if it departs from their trademark assertion that election is the ground of the Trinity. On this premise, the traditional idea of an antecedent Trinity appears as "abstract" and "speculative." However, not only does this idea cut the nerve of Barth's doctrine of revelation, it also leaves us with a clear choice about how to understand what counts as "abstract" and "speculative." Moreover, it also presents us a clear choice about how to understand the condition for the possibility of the incarnation—is it theological (as grounded in the eternal Trinity) or ontological (as grounded in the ontology of actualism)? Barth's revisers need to tell us why the "ontological" should be preferred to the "theological."

With the revisionists' explanatory thesis in view, we seem to have landed well within the precincts of $ontology_1$. A posteriori reasons grounded in revelation are no longer enough. An ontological scheme is needed if the incarnation is to be rendered intelligible (96). A distinct form of deductive reasoning has entered into the discussion. What the "actualistic ontology" would offer Barth is something he never wanted—a rationalistic basis for explaining the incarnation.

Revisionists and traditionalists can agree on a basic point. Barth did not view God's being in abstraction from his active relations. God's being was always in his activity, not over and above it. Furthermore, in a certain sense, both can agree that for Barth the concrete form of God's being was inseparable from a decision. Where revisionists and traditionalists part ways is over the nature of that decision. For the revisionists it was the pretemporal decision of election, whereas for the traditionalists it was God's prior generation of the Son by the Father in the unity of the Holy Spirit.

Both views might give us a "relational ontology," in the sense of ontology_2, because both could agree on the general point that God's being is always relational in nature. The revisionists, however, drive their actualism toward a version of ontology_1 by proposing it as a framework of rationalistic explanation. Moreover, they seem to believe that God's being would not be "concrete" and "determinate" without existing in relation to the world. Traditionalists would argue, by contrast, that for Barth God's being was already concrete and determinate, prior to election, by virtue of God's active trinitarian relations within the Godhead.

In short, whereas the traditionalists uphold Barth's doctrine of antecedence, the revisionists want to flip it over into a doctrine of subsequence. For the revisionists, God's trinitarian being is subsequent to God's relationship to the world. Election has the logical and ontological priority, apart from which the Trinity is merely potential or at least indeterminate. For the traditionalists, on the other hand, God's being in relation to the world is grounded in God's being in and for himself. The Trinity is always logically and ontologically antecedent. This, then, is the disputed question: Is God's eternal trinitarian being—for the later Barth—subsequent or antecedent to election?

Deductive Reasoning

Where does the idea of a thoroughly modern actualistic ontology come from? What gets it off the ground? The thesis of this study is that the revisionist position derives, not entirely, but to a large extent, from taking one of Barth's statements out of context, turning it into an abstract proposition, and deducing certain conclusions from it that Barth would not have drawn.

A seminal revisionist passage runs as follows:

> He [the eternal Logos] is *incarnandus* [the Word to be enfleshed] only as a result of the . . . decision [of election]; prior to making it, His being and existence are *undetermined*.

> If now Barth wishes to speak of Jesus Christ (and not an abstractly conceived Logos *asarkos*) as the Subject of election, he *must* deny to the Logos a mode or state of being above and prior to the decision to be incarnate in time.
>
> He *must*, to employ the traditional terminology, say that there is no Logos in and for himself in distinction from God's act of turning toward the world and humanity in predestination; the Logos is *incarnandus* in and for himself, in eternity.
>
> For that move alone *would* make it clear that it is "Jesus Christ" who is the Subject of election and not an indeterminate (or "absolute") Logos *asarkos*. (McCormack, "Grace and Being," 94–95, italics added)[13]

This complicated passage invites careful examination. I should note, however, that my analysis at this point is preliminary. The status of the Logos *asarkos* in the later Barth, along with related questions, will be considered more fully below. It bears mentioning at the outset, however, that in Barth the Logos *asarkos* never had the status of being merely an "abstraction." The Logos *asarkos* would be "abstract" in itself only on the premise that the antecedent Trinity was something abstract in itself. Reasons for regarding the antecedent Trinity as "concrete" have already been given. As late as IV/1 (as will be shown), Barth continued to regard the Logos *asarkos* as a reality whose status in itself was actual, determinate, and concrete. It is true, however, that some of Barth's statements are subtle and possibly misleading.[14]

Contrary to the revisionist claim, it is not God's pretemporal decision of election that makes the divine Logos "determinate." Because the antecedent eternal Trinity is already determinate in itself, the eternal

13. I have reformatted this passage to make it more followable. It appears as a single block in the original.

14. By way of anticipation, let me cite from John Webster, who I believe gets the subtlety right. In commenting on Barth's early exegesis of the prologue to John's Gospel, Webster writes, "So also in [John 1:2]: οὗτος [he] refers forward to Jesus Christ and his history, rather than backward to the Logos, so that the Logos is by definition *incarnandus*. But as Barth unfolds John's incarnational teaching, above all in John 1:14, it becomes clear that any such affirmation must not compromise the integrity of the Logos [as such], whose entire perfection is retained in the act of *Menschwerdung* [becoming human]." It is the "entire perfection" of the eternal Logos as a reality already determinate in itself prior to the incarnation that is at stake. See John Webster, "Barth's Lectures on the Gospel of John," in *Thy Word Is Truth: Barth on Scripture*, ed. George Hunsinger (Grand Rapids: Eerdmans, 2012), 142–43.

divine Logos is also determinate within it. It does not need a relationship to the world in order to become "determinate." Already determinate in itself, for Barth, the eternal divine Logos takes on a new and secondary determination in the pretemporal decision of election. In other words, as I will argue more fully below, by virtue of election the Logos *asarkos* becomes *also* the Logos *incarnandus* without ceasing to be the Logos *asarkos*. By definition, the one indivisible Logos is totally *asarkos* and totally *incarnandus/incarnatus* at the same time (*totus/totus*).[15]

The revisionist claim to the contrary does not rest heavily on textual evidence. It rests mainly on deductions derived from Barthian statements that are taken from their context and treated in isolation. That is what happens in the lengthy passage quoted above.

Note how the passage twice uses the word *must*. This appeal to logical necessity points to the deductive mode of reasoning behind the revisionist claim. If the inferences are unwarranted, the revisionist edifice will not stand. Along with neglecting the principle of charity (as yet to be examined), the inferences in this passage are the Achilles' heel of the new Barth-revisionism.

Consider the chain of the reasoning. If, as Barth states (and he does state this), "Jesus Christ is the Subject of election," then, we are told, Barth "*must* deny to the Logos a mode or state of being above and prior to the decision to be incarnate in time" (95, italics added). Why *must* he deny this? The conclusion here simply doesn't follow. We are looking at a non sequitur. Granted, the meaning of the statement "Jesus Christ is the Subject of election" needs to be unpacked, as will be done in due course. Nevertheless, there is no good reason to believe that the idea of a Logos *asarkos* is *necessarily* incompatible

15. For an example of how Barth uses the *totus/totus* scheme, see his great excursus on divine freedom, where he writes of God's being *totus intra et totus extra* with respect to the creature (II/1, 315). Since he held that God's being is indivisible, I am extending this scheme to how the Logos *asarkos* and the Logos *ensarkos* are related. This extension seems justified by his embrace of the *extra Calvinisticum* (see below), and by statements like the following: "Although in his eternal being and action towards the world God is undivided and indivisibly One and the Same—although he is always wholly the One he is—the mode of his action varies" (II/1, 315, rev.). Barth posits an "abundant variety" and "manifold richness" to the forms that God's presence can (and does) assume simultaneously (II/1, 319). In each of these multiple forms God is present as an indivisible whole.

with the statement that Jesus Christ is the Subject of election. No textual evidence is adduced in support of this claim. It is merely a matter of logical inference, and the inference is unwarranted. The Logos *asarkos*, as I will show, is presupposed in Barth's claim that Jesus Christ is the Subject of election.

The reasoning continues. "He *must* . . . say that there is no Logos in and for himself in distinction from God's act of turning toward the world and humanity in predestination" (95, italics added). Note that again no claim is being made that Barth *did* say this, which in fact he never did. The claim is rather that he "must" say it as a matter of logical necessity. But just why must he say it? While further reasons might be given, they simply do not add up, as will be seen. In fact Barth makes statements, even in II/2, whose natural meaning is that in the decision of election, the Logos freely determines himself anew, and that it is precisely the Logos "in and for himself" who does so, that is, the Logos who is already determinate as a member of the eternal Trinity. Again, we are looking at a deductive inference with no corroborating textual evidence. Recall again, for the moment, Barth's statement that Jesus Christ's identity as God's Son "of course does not rest on election" (II/2, 114).

Finally, notice the claim that only these revisionist inferences "*would* make it clear that it is 'Jesus Christ' who is the Subject of election and not an indeterminate (or 'absolute') Logos *asarkos*" (95, italics added). Here again we are confronted by a forced option. The Subject of election is said to be either Jesus Christ or else the Logos *asarkos*. No attempt is made to show why the one necessarily excludes the other (to say nothing of the claim that prior to election the divine Logos is supposedly "indeterminate"). Are there really no alternatives? Although the principle of charity would require that one entertain other possibilities—since on this basis it is going to be claimed that Barth is "inconsistent"—no alternative is ever considered. We are looking at a chain of inferences presented as if they were self-evident.

With these revisionist inferences in place, we come to the pivotal claim. Given that the *real* Barth is the logically inferred Barth, the other Barth—the one whom we actually encounter in the pages of the *Church Dogmatics*—can be said to suffer from "inconsistency." The actually existing textual Barth, as I will call him, stands in tension with the "real" Barth of the revisionists. It is the "real" Barth (i.e., the inferred Barth) who "must" discard not only the Logos *asarkos* but also every vestige of "essentialist ontology" in order to embrace a thoroughly modern "actualistic ontology." The merely textual Barth *would* have embraced this metaphysically purified ontology if only he had taken pains to be more consistent. The inferred Barth is the gold standard against which the actually existing Barth comes up wanting. The deduced entity is used to claim that the textual Barth is inconsistent.

The revisionists concede that the actually existing textual Barth never carried this metaphysical program through to completion. That is why they feel moved "*to register a critical correction.*" They propose to remove what they perceive as a deep "*inconsistency in Barth's thought*" (102, italics added). It is their project of straightening Barth out that makes them revisionists. They propose to revise Barth so that he will no longer be inconsistent.

Barth's newly minted doctrine of election (as the revisionists interpret it) logically requires that he pursue a "postmetaphysical" theology purged of all "classical metaphysics." Unfortunately, Barth himself seems to have dropped the ball. As far as the revisionists are able to discover, he never satisfactorily corrected his views. To their abiding regret, "*no retractions were ever offered*" (102, italics added).

The revisionists admit—and this is a major concession—that in fact Barth never reversed the order of the Trinity and election (102). Speaking for the revisionists—who have now enlisted a whole team of younger scholars—Professor McCormack confesses:

> The only conclusion I have been able to come to is that Barth either did not fully realize the profound *implications* of his doctrine of election for the doctrine of the Trinity, or he shied away from drawing them for reasons known only to himself.[16] (102, italics added)

In effect, this statement asserts that one of the most accomplished theologians of our time lacked the wherewithal (whether mental or volitional) to carry his insights through to completion. The traditionalists, by contrast, believe that Barth was perfectly capable of revising his ideas whenever he thought it was necessary.

16. Note that this borders on being an ad hominem argument.

There is a difference between ambiguity and inconsistency. At points where Barth may be ambiguous, the revisionists tend to draw him in their direction. They view the resulting Barth as the real Barth. This Barth is then used to claim that he is inconsistent whenever he runs counter—as he often does—to what the revisionists believe he ought to have said. No attempt is made to resolve the perceived inconsistencies. Instead the revisionists feel entitled to discount whatever does not fit with the Barth of their controlling ontology. At the same time, they tend to read their view of Barth into passages that will not sustain it when examined carefully. Examples will be presented as we proceed.

An initial idea can now be gathered about why the counterevidence counts for so little to the revisionists. They simply harbor no doubts about the validity of their logical inferences, which they then use as a hermeneutical norm. On the basis of their inferences, they claim that Barth's theology is "inconsistent" as it stands. In other words, the inferred Barth is inconsistent with the actually existing textual Barth. However, if what Barth "must" have meant should turn out to be unfounded, then the new, improved Barth would be a misconception. All that is solid for the revisionists would melt into air.

Extra Calvinisticum

The "Grace and Being" essay includes an important excursus on "the *extra Calvinisticum*" (95–101). *Extra Calvinisticum* is a technical term given by Lutheran scholastic theologians in the seventeenth century to the Calvinistic teaching that Christ's divine nature cannot merely be enclosed within a human nature but remains infinite despite being in union with a finite body. Admittedly this is a technical matter, but it casts important light on the revisionist position. Almost all of the excursus—which contains many valid points—is admirably carried out. The problem with it, however, is signaled by the title: "Barth's Critique of the *extra Calvinisticum*" (95). Although Barth was certainly critical of this idea, he was not merely critical. He also had a more positive estimation that is unfortunately discounted.

Before proceeding, it may be useful to recognize some of the many admirable points in the "Grace and Being" essay, especially in the excursus. The author rightly sees that Barth's doctrine of election is perhaps the high point of the *Church Dogmatics*. He understands that for Barth God's election is an act of free grace. In accord with Barth he does not wish to affirm any other God than the one revealed in the history of Jesus Christ. He sees that for Barth we can only know God's being by grace through faith as we acknowledge God's revelation in his Word and through his Spirit. He admits that for Barth God as Creator, Reconciler, and Redeemer is none other in his works than he is in himself. He agrees that for Barth God is never dependent upon us in any way. He affirms that the economic Trinity and the immanent Trinity are identical in content. He sees that for Barth God is the Lord over his being and essence. He affirms with Barth that the Logos *incarnandus* is at once *asarkos* and *ensarkos*— "*asarkos* (because not yet embodied) and *ensarkos* (by way of anticipation, on the basis of God's self-determination in the act of electing)." He continues that "the Logos *incarnatus* is both *asarkos* (the so-called '*extra-Calvinisticum*') and *ensarkos* (having become embodied)" (67–68). On all these points the traditionalists would have no disagreement with Professor McCormack. They might differ, however, on what some of these statements mean.

What invites our attention in the excursus is the decisive point about how Barth understands the Logos *asarkos* in relation to the Logos *incarnandus*. How does Barth think the divine Logos as the "second person" of the Trinity (the Logos *asarkos*) is related to the divine Logos as determined for election and incarnation (the Logos *incarnandus*)? We already know the revisionist answer. The two are identical in every respect. There is no "second person" of the Trinity, no Logos *asarkos*, who is not already "constituted" as the Logos *incarnandus*, so that the Trinity knows no Logos *asarkos* in and for itself. The Logos was always slated to become incarnate, having no other raison d'être in the Godhead, and once the Logos has become *incarnatus* (incarnate), it can no longer be *asarkos* at the same time. These ideas are thought to follow from the proposition that election is the ground of the Trinity.

What the excursus permits us to see is how revisionism interprets certain relevant Barthian texts. For the sake of clarity, it will be helpful to begin with a passage not treated in the "Grace and Being" essay. From there we can turn to some that are.

An indication of how the later Barth viewed the Logos *asarkos* appears in III/1. (Note that this is well after II/2.) In III/1 Barth discusses the role of the Logos *asarkos* in the eternal Trinity prior to election and the incarnation. From there he takes up the question of how the Logos *asarkos* is related to God's work as directed outside himself in the creation (his *opus ad extra externum*). Barth's account in III/1 proceeds in two steps: he discusses first the Logos *asarkos* in itself, then the Logos as it relates to the incarnation. Although there is only one Logos, it subsists simultaneously in these two states of being.

The Logos *asarkos*, for Barth, is primordial and perpetual. It has an indispensable role to play within the inner life of the eternal Trinity. It not only is logically and ontologically prior to the incarnation but also persists over against and along with the incarnation. Relative to the incarnation, the Logos *asarkos* is known as the *extra Calvinisticum*. It indicates that aspect of the eternal Logos that retains its primordial role within the inner life of the eternal Trinity once the Logos has also become enfleshed. Although Barth rejected the *extra Calvinisticum* in certain respects, he did not reject it in this primordial and perpetual respect.

The Logos *asarkos* in its primordial aspect is described as follows: "It is legitimate and imperative that by the expression 'Son' or 'Word of God' we should here understand the *second mode of existence* ('person') of the *inner* divine reality *in itself* and *as such*" (III/1, 50; italics original, here restored). In this statement Barth affirms, as he always does in the *Church Dogmatics*, that the antecedent Trinity is something that enjoys "an *inner* . . . reality *in itself* and *as such*" (italics original). In other words, the Trinity (and each "person" within it) is determinate prior to God's dealings with the world. The Word of God (the Logos *asarkos*) belongs to the Trinity's inner divine reality and needs no external relationship to make it become determinate.

Barth then introduces one of his typical points about the eternal Trinity. "God is not alone in himself but is the eternal begetter of the Son, who is the eternally begotten of the Father." No mention is yet made of election and the incarnation. This eternal begetting is assumed to be prior to and independent of the incarnation (as in all traditional ecumenical theology). God is not alone, because as the eternal Trinity he is already a God of love and freedom in himself.

The Father loves the Son, and the Son loves the Father, in the unity of the Holy Spirit, to all eternity (III/1, 50).

God's inner triune life "in itself and as such" is then set forth as the *ground* of God's subsequent dealings with the world. "In the same freedom and love in which God is not alone in himself but is the eternal begetter of the Son . . . he *also* turns as Creator *ad extra*" (III/1, 50, italics added). In light of the debate about election and the Trinity, the word *also* here should not be overlooked. It can often be of substantive importance to Barth.[17] It indicates that the freedom and love that the triune God enjoys in himself is the basis on which he *also* turns, in that same freedom and love, to be the Creator of that which is outside himself. God's antecedent reality as the Trinity is the logical and ontological ground of his secondary identity as the Creator. As Athanasius and the Cappadocians would put it, the Father/Son relation is prior to the Creator/creature relation.

Barth then draws a comparison between God's inner trinitarian life and his life in relation to the world. "*Just as* God in himself is neither deaf nor dumb but speaks and hears his Word from all eternity, *so also* [*auch*] outside his eternity he does not wish to be without hearing or echo, that is, without the ears and voices of the creature" (III/1, 50, rev.; italics added).[18] The particular Word that God hears in eternity is, in the first and primary instance, the Logos *asarkos*, the Word begotten eternally by the Father, the Word who has not yet become incarnate, and whose role in the Godhead is not reducible to his being appointed to become incarnate (as the Logos *incarnandus*).

It might be noted here that the transition from the Logos *asarkos* to the Logos *incarnandus* is not a "two-act drama." It is rather a matter of one eternal act with two aspects. There is no disagreement at this point between the traditionalists and the revisionists.[19] The

17. The word *also* (*auch*) does this kind of conceptual work throughout Barth's dogmatics. For another example, see William T. Barnett, "Actualism and Beauty: Karl Barth's Insistence on the *Auch* in His Account of Divine Beauty," *Scottish Journal of Theology* 66 (2013): 299–318.

18. The world *also* (*auch*) is dropped from this sentence in the English translation. For the German original, see Barth, *Kirchliche Dogmatik*, vol. III, part 1 (Zurich: Theologische Verlag Zurich, 1945), 53.

19. Professor McCormack would ascribe the "two act" view to the traditionalists. See Bruce L. McCormack, "Processions and Missions: A Point of Convergence between

disagreement pertains rather to the status of the eternal act's two aspects with regard to the Logos *asarkos*. Unlike the revisionists, the traditionalists deny that for Barth the Logos *asarkos* is absorbed into the incarnation without remainder. They believe that for Barth the Logos continues to transcend the incarnation even while totally partaking in it. As mentioned, this transcendent aspect of the Logos is what has traditionally been called the *extra Calvinisticum*.[20]

What, then, is the relationship between the triune God's eternal fellowship in himself and the fellowship he establishes with the creature? Just as it was in I/1, and just as it will be again, for example, in IV/2, the relationship in III/1 is explicitly described as one of "correspondence." The revisionists would claim that after II/2 this "correspondence" language disappears.[21] It doesn't. But they need it to disappear if they are to validate their grounding of the eternal Trinity in the economic Trinity, or the processions in the missions—that is, if they are to carry out a reversal from antecedence to subsequence as required by their "actualistic ontology." Here is another place where the revisionist Barth is at variance with the actually existing textual Barth—that is, a place where Barth would have to be seen as "inconsistent."

Note what the textual Barth actually says: "The eternal fellowship between Father and Son, *or between God and His Word*, thus finds a *correspondence* in the very different but not dissimilar fellowship between God and his creature" (III/1, 50, italics added). The relationship between who and what the triune God is in himself and who and what he is in relation to the creation is one of *correspondence*, not

---

Thomas Aquinas and Karl Barth," in *Thomas Aquinas and Karl Barth: An Unofficial Catholic-Protestant Dialogue*, ed. Bruce L. McCormack and Thomas Joseph White (Grand Rapids: Eerdmans, 2013), 20.

20. The standard discussion is still E. David Willis, *Calvin's Catholic Christology: The Function of the So-Called Extra Calvinisticum in Calvin's Theology* (Leiden: E. J. Brill, 1966).

21. Barth is thought to include—by nature not by grace—the Trinity's temporal missions in its eternal divine processions, thereby "eliminating" the "analogical gap" (i.e., the ontological divide) between the economic Trinity and the immanent Trinity, or between the missions and the processions (or, in effect, it would seem, between time and eternity). This move turns the actually existing textual Barth on his head. See McCormack, "Processions and Missions," 115–16.

(as it apparently is with the revisionists) one of dialectical identity.[22] The relationship is asymmetrical and irreversible. In this passage from III/1, the former (the eternal Trinity) is specified as the ground of the latter (the economic Trinity), as the traditionalists would claim over against the revisionists.

Barth concludes this line of thought: "It [God's turning to the world as the Creator] is in keeping with the Father of the eternal Son, the One who speaks *the eternal Word as such*; it is wholly worthy of him, that in his dealings *ad extra* he should be the Creator. This is one understanding of the function of the Son or Word of God in this matter" (III/1, 50, italics added). The Son or the Word of God is thought to have more than one function. There can be no doubt that Barth is speaking here about the Logos *asarkos* as subsisting in the eternal Trinity with a role independent of election and the incarnation. Although this role is not the Word's only role, for Barth it is nonetheless inalienable and enduring.

Some related material appears in IV/2, which is again in line with the traditionalist view. As has been the case ever since I/1, Barth continues to see the relationship between the economic Trinity and the immanent Trinity as one of "correspondence."

> The triune life of God . . . is the *basis* of [God's] whole will and action even *ad extra*. . . . It is the *basis* of his *decretum et opus ad extra* [election and creation], of the relationship which he has . . . established with a reality which is distinct from himself. . . . It [the triune life] is the *basis* of the election of man to covenant with himself; of the determination of the Son to become man, and therefore to fulfill this covenant. (IV/2, 345, italics added)

22. By "dialectical identity," I mean the idea of looking at one self-identical object from two different but mutually exclusive perspectives. An example would be a figure/ground drawing where when you see a vase you don't see two faces looking at each other, and when you see the two faces you don't see the vase. Another example would be Wittgenstein's duck/rabbit. The difference between God's self-relationship and God's world-relationship is not a matter of two different perspectives on one and the same self-identical reality. That would also hold true of the relationship between the economic Trinity and the immanent Trinity, between the missions and the processions, or, indeed, between time and eternity. These relationships for Barth are always a matter of asymmetrical unity-in-distinction, not of dialectical identity.

> And *because* he is the God of triune life, he does not will and do anything strange by so doing. In it [God's turning to the world in Christ] he [the triune God] lives in the *repetition and confirmation* of what he is in himself. What then . . . is the distance, the confrontation, the encounter and the partnership between himself and the world, himself and [the human creature], but a representation, reflection and *correspondence* of the distinction with which he is *in himself* the Father and the Son? (IV/2, 346, italics added)

In this material from IV/2, Barth states clearly that the eternal Trinity—as something determinate and sufficient in itself—is the basis on which God turns toward the world. The revisionist demurral would again have to be that in making these statements Barth continues to display his inconsistency. And revisionism is right to the extent that once again the actually existing textual Barth is incompatible with the postulate of a postmetaphysical Barth.

This may be as good a place as any to flag how the charge of inconsistency functions. In effect, it renders the revisionist claims irrefutable. When inconvenient passages like those just examined from III/1 and IV/2 are adduced, it only goes to show that Barth was not always consistent. In this way revisionism cannot be falsified. No matter what the counterevidence may be, it can always be chalked up to inconsistency. Much depends in the end, of course, on whether revisionism has rightly interpreted Barth's statement that Jesus Christ is the Subject of election, a question yet to be explored. Nevertheless, counterevidence such as I have just presented casts doubt on the claim that the later Barth adopted an actualistic ontology according to which it follows that the Logos *asarkos* is indeterminate prior to election, that election is the ground of the Trinity, and that the language of trinitarian "repetition" and "correspondence" disappears.[23]

23. For the claim that the later Barth eliminates the "ontological gap" or radical difference between the historical and the eternal Trinity, and thus between the incarnate Word and the eternal Word, thereby eliminating the idea of a "correspondence" between them (apparently in favor of something like "dialectical identity"), see McCormack, *Orthodox and Modern*, 217. To make this claim work, however, the proviso must be attached that "Barth was not always consistent—even in II/2" (ibid., 217n). Once again, this is special pleading.

Having established (in passages written after II/2) his main point that the Trinity itself is the ground of election and the creation—"the *basis* of his *decretum et opus ad extra*" (IV/2, 345)—Barth goes on to work out some of its ramifications. When the New Testament writers spoke about God's "Word," he asks, what exactly did they have in mind? Did they mean the Logos *asarkos*, "the second person of the Trinity in itself and as such" (III/1, 54)? That is, did they mean "the eternal Son (or eternal Word) of God in his pure deity" (III/1, 54)? Or rather, "more inclusively and more concretely," did they not in fact mean "the Son of God as the Son of Man, the Word made flesh" (III/1, 54)? Even when they spoke simply about the Word (as in the prologue to the Gospel of John), Barth suggests, what they actually had in mind was not the Logos *asarkos* in itself and as such but instead the Word of God incarnate. If so, can the traditionalist view be sustained?

In a way that seems to accord with the revisionists, Barth goes on in III/1 to describe the Logos *asarkos* as an "abstraction." "It has to be kept in mind," he cautions, "that the whole conception of the λόγος ἄσαρκος [Logos *asarkos*], the 'second person' of the Trinity as such, is an abstraction" (III/1, 54). In what sense does he think it is an abstraction? Much depends, as we will see, on the answer to this question. For now it need only be indicated that the answer is not self-evident. We will return to it shortly.

It should not be overlooked that Barth immediately adds a qualification: "It is true that it [the idea of the Logos *asarkos*] has shown itself necessary to the christological and trinitarian reflections of the Church. Even today it is indispensable for dogmatic enquiry and presentation" (III/1, 54). In what sense is it still indispensable? What status does Barth finally ascribe to this idea? Again, this is an important question to which we will need to return.

Barth offers at least this clue:

> The New Testament speaks plainly enough about *the Jesus Christ who existed before the world was*, but always was with a view to the *concrete* content of the eternal divine will and decree. For this reason it does not speak expressly of the eternal Son or Word as such, but of the Mediator, the One who *in the eternal sight of God* has *already*

> taken upon himself our human nature, i.e., not of a formless Christ who might well be a Christ-principle or something of that kind, but of *Jesus the Christ*. (III/1, 54, italics added)

Here the word *concrete* undeniably pertains to God's eternal decree of election. It is because of the pretemporal decree of election that the New Testament rarely speaks expressly (if at all) of the Logos *asarkos* (or the eternal Son) in itself and as such. Instead it speaks "concretely" (or, perhaps, as we read earlier, "more concretely") about the Mediator, that is, about the incarnate Word. The New Testament does not speak about "a formless Christ who might well be a Christ-principle or something of that kind" (III/1, 54). Instead, to prevent all misunderstanding, it speaks concretely about Jesus the Christ, the *Logos ensarkos* (the enfleshed Word) and, by implication, the Logos *incarnandus* (the eternal Word appointed to become incarnate), who somehow "existed before the world was."

The traditionalist view must obviously reckon with these statements. It cannot sidestep them or brush them aside. It must take them in context and interpret them. It must explain how these secondary ramifications are not inconsistent with what Barth said so clearly at the outset of the same passage in III/1 when establishing his first and main point that the antecedent Trinity (and thus the Logos *asarkos*) enjoys "an inner . . . reality in itself and as such" (III/1, 50). Let it be openly admitted that while the main point seems congenial to the traditionalists, the secondary ramifications do not, at least not at first. Must the traditionalist view finally fail on account of these secondary ramifications? Can it show that Barth still grants an ongoing status, as it claims, to the Logos *asarkos* over and above the Logos *incarnandus*?

It must not be overlooked that Barth points to "the One who in the eternal sight of God has already taken upon himself our human nature" (III/1, 54). What does he mean here by "the eternal sight of God"? Elsewhere in III/1 he makes a similar remark about what counts as "concrete" when he states,

> If by the Son or the Word of God we understand *concretely* Jesus, the Christ, and therefore very God and very man, *as he existed in the counsel of God from all eternity and before creation*, we can see how far it was not only appropriate and worthy but necessary that God

should be the Creator. If this was God's *eternal counsel* in the freedom of his love, the counsel *actualized* in the manger of Bethlehem, the cross of Calvary and the tomb of Joseph of Arimathea, it was not merely possible but essential for God to be the Creator. The fact that God has regard to his Son—the Son of Man, the Word made flesh—is the true and genuine basis of creation. To be sure *there was no other necessity than that of his own free love.* But a genuine necessity is constituted by the fact from all eternity he willed so to love the world, and did so love it, that he gave his only begotten Son (John 3:16). (III/1, 51, italics added)

Again, much depends on what Barth means when he states that the Word had "*already*" taken upon himself our human nature "*in the eternal sight of God*" (III/1, 54, italics added). Likewise, much depends on what he means when he refers to "*the counsel of God from all eternity and before creation*" according to which "Jesus, the Christ, and therefore very God and very man" *already existed concretely* in pretemporal eternity (III/1, 51, italics added). How are we to understand these important references to the "eternal sight of God" and the "eternal counsel of God"? What does Barth mean when he speaks about understanding the Logos *concretely* and thus (let it be openly acknowledged) about the Logos *incarnandus* and the Logos *incarnatus*?

Before entering into these questions more fully, two other matters will be broached. They concern issues that are mentioned in Professor McCormack's excursus regarding the *extra Calvinisticum.*

In the "Grace and Being" excursus a passage from IV/1 is cited and discussed. It will be quoted here more fully for the sake of clarity. Barth writes,

The first and eternal Word of God, which *underlies and precedes* the creative will and work as the beginning of all things in God, means in fact Jesus Christ. It is identical with the One who, very God and very man, born and living and acting and suffering and conquering in time, accomplishes the atonement. It is he alone who is the content and form of the gracious thought and will and resolve of God in relation to the world and man before ever these were and as God willed and created them. (IV/1, 51–52, italics added)

When Barth writes here about "the beginning of all things in God," he means the beginning of all things external to God in the creation. When the New Testament refers to the Word of God in this connection, Barth suggests it in fact means Jesus Christ. It does not mean the Logos *asarkos* in and of itself. The first and eternal Word of God, the Logos *asarkos*, is said to be "identical" with the incarnate Son, that is, with the Logos *incarnatus* (and by implication with the Logos *incarnandus* as well).

We need to ask whether this identity relation between the *Logos asarkos* and the Logos *incarnandus/incarnatus* is meant *simpliciter* (without qualification) or only *secundum quid* (in a certain respect). The answer emerges as the passage in IV/1 unfolds. But so far what we have seen is this: for Barth, when it comes to God's relationship to the world and humankind from all eternity, it is *not* the Logos *asarkos* but Jesus Christ *alone* whom God has in view—in his eternal sight and counsel—before these (the world and humankind) ever existed and before God ever created them (even though, as Barth says, this counsel is not "actualized" until the incarnation).

Jesus Christ, the incarnate Son (Logos *ensarkos*)—or we might say more simply, Jesus of Nazareth—was already present to God in pretemporal eternity. This is certainly an amazing statement. In what sense does Barth think he can say this? While the answer is implicit, it does not immediately emerge. Only as Barth proceeds does he make what is implicit to be more explicit.

He continues,

> In this context we must not refer to the second "person" of the Trinity as such, to the eternal Son or the eternal Word of God *in abstracto*, and therefore to the so-called λόγος ἄσαρκος. What is the point of a regress to him *as the supposed basis of the being and knowledge of all things*? In any case, how can we make such a regress?
>
> The second "person" of the Godhead in himself and as such is not God the Reconciler. *In himself and as such he* [the second person of the Godhead] *is not revealed to us*. In himself and as such he is not *Deus pro nobis*, either ontologically or epistemologically. He is the content of *a necessary and important concept* in trinitarian doctrine when we have to understand the revelation and dealings of God in the light of *their free basis in the inner being and essence of God*.

> But since we are now concerned with the revelation and dealings of God, and particularly with the atonement, with the person and work of the Mediator, it is pointless, as it is impermissible, to return to the inner being and essence of God and especially to the second person of the Trinity *as such*, in such a way that we ascribe to this person another form than that which God himself has given in willing *to reveal himself and to act outwards.*
>
> If it is true that God became man, then in this we have to recognize and respect his eternal will and purpose and resolve—*his free and gracious will which he did not owe it either to himself or to the world to have*, by which he did not need to come to the decision to which he has in fact come, and *behind which, in these circumstances, we cannot go*, behind which we do not have to reckon with any Son of God in himself, with any λόγος ἄσαρκος, with any other Word of God than that which was made flesh.
>
> According to the free and gracious will of God, the eternal Son of God is Jesus Christ as he lived and died and rose again in time, and none other. (IV/1, 52, italics added)[24]

We begin by noting that Barth understands himself to be speaking in a particular context (*secundum quid*). He is not speaking here about God's being in and of itself (though, as we will see, he does offer a remarkable aside concerning it). The particular context in question is God's relationship to the world, not God's inner trinitarian life. God's relationship *to the world* is determined from all eternity by Jesus Christ alone, who, according to Barth, is in some mysterious way already present to God (to his eternal sight and counsel) prior to the act of creation at the beginning of all things.

In this context it would be a mistake—indeed an *abstraction*—to operate with the idea of the Logos *asarkos*. When it comes to God's relationship to the world, it is not a matter of "the eternal Son or the eternal Word of God *in abstracto*, and therefore [of] the so-called λόγος ἄσαρκος" (IV/1, 52). In the passage as it unfolds, Barth gives us reason to believe that he is not rejecting the idea of the Logos *asarkos* absolutely but only in a certain respect.[25]

24. I have reformatted this dense but very important passage, which appears in the original as one single block, in the hope of making it more followable.

25. Although I share John Webster's substantive concerns, I think he is too hasty in dismissing Barth's use of "abstraction" in this context, which is rather narrower

The Logos *asarkos* is indeed presupposed by election and the incarnation, but in this context it is present only in the background. It is a kind of unaccented syllable. If we were to remove this unaccented syllable from its embeddedness in a larger and richer context in order to work with it separately or directly, we would in fact be engaging in an abstraction. It would be a mistake to take it out of the background and put it into the foreground to the expense of all else. Because of God's pretemporal decision of election, the Logos *asarkos* in itself and as such is not relevant to God's relationship to the world. Without ceasing to exist as such, it has been determined (and has determined itself) to be the Logos *ensarkos* and therefore to be Jesus Christ. It is Jesus Christ alone, mysteriously present in some sense from all eternity—a sense we will later need to explain—who establishes all God's ways and works with the world.

It is clear from this section of IV/1 (as also from III/1, 51–54) that Barth has a special worry about taking the Logos *asarkos* out of its context in God's inner trinitarian life and using it to think directly about the triune God's relations with the world in his identity as Creator, Reconciler, and Redeemer. If the Logos *asarkos* were the salient factor in these relations and not the Logos *ensarkos*, then the door would be wide open to natural theology, something (as is well-known) Barth wishes to avoid at all costs.[26] It would (*per impossible*) be operative independently of and alongside Jesus Christ. The Logos *asarkos*—not Jesus Christ himself and Jesus Christ alone—could then easily and unhappily be mistaken as "the supposed basis of the being and knowledge of all things" external to God (IV/1, 52). For Barth, that basis is Christ alone, not the Logos *asarkos* as such.

Beginning with Christian apologists in the second century (like Justin Martyr and Clement of Alexandria) all the way down to modern

and more subtle than Webster allows. See John Webster, "Trinity and Creation," *International Journal of Systematic Theology* 12 (2010): 4–19; on 17–18n40.

26. For a brilliant account of why Barth rejected natural theology—and especially of what he saw as its nefarious political implications during the struggle against Nazism—see Mark R. Lindsay, *Reading Auschwitz with Barth: The Holocaust as Problem and Promise for Barthian Theology* (Eugene, OR: Pickwick, 2013), 64–89. See also Kevin Diller, *Theology's Epistemological Dilemma: How Karl Barth and Alvin Plantinga Provide a Unified Response* (Downers Grove, IL: IVP Academic, 2014), 177–222.

times (in many and various ways), the Logos *asarkos* has regularly been invoked in Barth's "abstract" sense—and sometimes with the unacceptable consequences against which he warns. That is one reason (but not the only reason) why Barth wishes to banish "the Logos *asarkos* as such" from this context.

When it comes to God's relations with the world, we cannot go behind God's pretemporal decision of election. Therefore neither can we go behind the mysterious presence of Jesus Christ himself in eternity at the beginning of all things, that is, at the beginning of all God's ways and works with the world. In this context it has to be recognized that "the eternal Son of God *is* Jesus Christ as he lived and died and rose again in time, and none other" (IV/1, 52, italics added).

But is this for Barth the only relevant context? Is there not perhaps also another? This passage gives us every reason to think that there is indeed another. Barth makes this astonishing claim: "The second 'person' of the Godhead in himself and as such is not God the Reconciler. In himself and as such he is not revealed to us. In himself and as such he is not *Deus pro nobis*, either ontologically or epistemologically" (IV/1, 52). This passage clearly suggests that the Logos *asarkos* in himself and as such still functions within the inner divine life of the Trinity.[27] The triune God still has a life of his own, in and for himself, to all eternity. In that sense the incarnate Logos does not exclude but includes the *extra Calvinisticum*.

The one undivided God is totally involved in his relations with the world, including his work and presence as the Reconciler. But in his inner trinitarian life as such, he is not the Reconciler. We have no access to God's inner trinitarian life as such. We know its terms (on the basis of revelation) but do not have access to its mysterious content.[28]

27. Barth's statement that the second person of the Godhead as such is not revealed to us is compatible with similar statements made elsewhere. "The Word as such," he writes, for example, "is before and above all created realities. It stands completely outside the series of created things. It precedes all being and all time. It is like God himself" (II/2, 95). The Word never loses this primordial status even though it enhances itself, so to speak, by also becoming the Logos *ensarkos*.

28. This is the standard ecumenical view. "The 'how' of God's act of existence [as the Holy Trinity] cannot be the passive object of human scrutiny," as Kahled Anatolios writes with respect to Athanasius. See Anatolios, *Retrieving Nicaea: The*

God's inner trinitarian life, in itself and as such, is not revealed to us. We know that God enjoys such an inner life, but we do not know what it is like because his unique divine life is unlike any life that we know. It is not properly communicable to created intellects. In order for us to know what it is like, we would have to be a second God.

The main point here is this: God indeed lives totally in and for the world, but God's life is not exhausted by his relationship to the world. To say that God is never unrelated to his creatures is not the same thing as saying that God is related only to his creatures. God's relationship in and for himself is distinct from his relationship to the world.[29] The first relationship is necessary (or noncontingent) while the second is contingent (or non-necessary), even though both relationships subsist in one and the same undivided divine act. That is the point of Barth's discourse, that God exists not only in and for himself as the Holy Trinity but *also* in relation to the world.

As noted, Professor McCormack is correct when he argues that we are looking at "one event with two terms," not "a two-act drama in pretemporal eternity." What he overlooks in his interpretation of Barth, however, is the noncontingency of the first term (God's inner trinitarian life) and the non-necessity of the second (God's life in relation to the world). For Barth, the one indivisible act in which God eternally subsists is internally differentiated along these lines.

Without these distinctions the temporal missions of the Trinity cannot be rightly distinguished from their eternal processions. The missions would begin to appear as if they were just as necessary to God as the processions. That may have been true, perhaps, for someone like Hegel, but not for Aquinas or Barth. It is incorrect to say that the relation between the missions and the processions, for the later Barth, is not a matter of correspondence and therefore not

---

Development and Meaning of Trinitarian Doctrine (Grand Rapids: Baker Academic, 2011), 141.

29. Although there are really no analogies, perhaps the following may be ventured. Small children are sometimes known to object if their parents want to go out together for an evening on their own. The child does not really grasp that the parents have a life together apart from their relationship to the child. While the parents may be fully invested in their relationship to the child, that does not mean they are not also fully invested in their own relationship apart from the child. The child knows only about the one and can have no real inkling of the other.

essentially analogical (as if it were perhaps a matter of dialectical identity instead).[30]

Along with his life in relation to the world, the triune God also lives totally in and for himself. Within the eternal God's inner trinitarian life, the Logos still subsists *concretely* as the Logos *asarkos*. To borrow words from Barth appearing in another context, the Logos *asarkos* is still "real in God in a form which is concealed from us and incomprehensible to us" (II/1, 357). In the eternal God's inner life, the Logos *asarkos*—although concealed from us and incomprehensible to us—is nonetheless abidingly real for God. "The eternal Logos is the Word in which God speaks with himself, thinks himself and is conscious of himself" to all eternity, not only in relation to the world but also first of all in and for himself (III/2, 147). The Logos *asarkos* subsists primordially and perpetually, not provisionally and transiently. That is what Barth means to establish, I submit, in these remarkable statements about the Logos who is not revealed to us (IV/1, 52). The Logos *asarkos* remains real in God in a hidden and incomprehensible form. It subsists eternally as the *extra Calvinisticum*.

The revisionists, who know about these statements, are flummoxed by them. How could the later Barth still find himself writing about "a second 'person' of the Godhead in himself and as such"? How could he possibly make room for a Logos *asarkos* or a pre-incarnate Son who is "not God the Reconciler"? How could Barth possibly refer to a "second person" of the Trinity who "in himself and as such . . . is not revealed to us"? What could possibly prompt him to think that there is a pre-incarnate Son who "in himself and as such . . . is not *Deus pro nobis*, either ontologically or epistemologically"? For the postmetaphysical Barth, what room could there possibly be for taking

30. See McCormack, "Processions and Missions" (*supra* n19), 114, 116, 118, 126. Professor McCormack writes: "If it is true that there is one eternal act with two terms, then the meaning of words like 'necessity' and 'freedom' *must* condition each other because both are defined by the one act" (ibid., 118n54; italics added). This conclusion is again a non sequitur, reflecting a rationalistic mode of reasoning. Note the reappearance of the telling word *must*. Mutual conditioning as posited here could not easily avoid the idea of mutual conditioning between God and the world—the highest stage (as we will see) of the revisionism's "actualistic ontology." Words like *necessity* and *freedom* cannot be dispensed with in theology, because they (or something like them) are required by the subject matter itself.

the Logos *asarkos* as "the content of a necessary and important concept in trinitarian doctrine" (IV/1, 52)?[31]

Instead of sending the revisionists back to the drawing board, these statements leave them scratching their heads. "What context," they wonder, "could there possibly be which would ever justify speaking in this way?" ("Grace and Being," 102). Having painted themselves into a corner with their rationalistic inferences, they can only imagine that Barth must have suffered from a "lapse of concentration" (102).[32] Clearly, these statements from IV/1 can only mean one thing. There is an "inconsistency in Barth's thought" that cries out to be removed (102). It never occurs to the revisionists to ask whether it is not Barth who is inconsistent with himself but rather the actually existing textual Barth who is indeed inconsistent—not with himself but with the fabricated Barth of their own devising. It does not occur to them that there might really be an ongoing place in the later Barth for a robust *extra Calvinisticum*.

For these reasons it is not possible to agree that for the later Barth "there is no Logos *asarkos* in the absolute sense of a mode of existence in the second 'person' of the Trinity which is independent of the determination for incarnation" (100). Barth's doctrine of election nuanced but did not reject this view of the Logos *asarkos*. The Logos *asarkos* was indeed "independent" of election and the incarnation—by nature, but not by grace.

Nor did Barth regard the Logos *asarkos* as something "speculative" in itself. He did not fear that "if we were to posit the existence of a Logos *asarkos* above and prior to the eternal decision to become incarnate in time, . . . we would be inviting speculation about the being and existence of the Logos in such a state or mode of being" (95). The idea of the Logos *asarkos* in itself was not "the kind of speculation his mature doctrine of election sought to eliminate" (101). As we have

31. It is a weakness in an otherwise fine study that Darren O. Sumner overlooks these important statements from IV/1, 51–52. Consequently he underestimates the continuity running from the early Barth of the *Göttingen Dogmatics* on through to the later Barth of IV/1 with regard to the *extra Calvinisticum*. See Sumner, "The Twofold Life of the Word: Karl Barth's Critical Reception of the *Extra Calvinisticum*," *International Journal of Systematic Theology* 15 (2013): 42–57.

32. This argument borders on contravening "the principle of humanity" as described at the outset of this study.

seen, Barth believed that the Logos *asarkos* as such and in itself was not merely speculative. It played a primordial and perpetual role in the inner life of the antecedent Trinity, even though "in himself and as such [the Logos *asarkos*] is not revealed to us" (IV/1, 52).[33] This role of the Logos *asarkos* in God's antecedent life was presupposed by election, not annulled by it. It is true, however, that epistemologically the Logos *asarkos* provided no basis for the knowledge of the antecedent Trinity. Any supposed knowledge of God on that basis would indeed be speculative.

Finally, it is not true that Barth worried about Calvin's version of the *extra Calvinisticum* because he feared it might lead to an "indeterminate" understanding of the Logos "above and prior to the determination to enter time and become human" (97). Barth's worries about Calvin lay elsewhere. He worried that Calvin's doctrine of election was "speculative" because it led to an abstract eternal decree (*decretum absolutum*) that was not properly informed by Christ and the Trinity. To see why leads us into our next section.

Speculation

We have one last matter to consider before moving on from "Grace and Being." With reference to the *extra Calvinisticum*, Barth writes,

> There is something regrettable about that theory [the *extra Calvinisticum*] insofar as it could lead, as it has to the present day, to *disastrous speculation* about a being and activity of a Logos *asarkos* and, therefore, about a God who could be known and whose divine essence could be defined on some other basis than in and from the perception of his presence and action as incarnate Word. And it cannot be denied that *Calvin himself* (with especially serious consequences in his doctrine of predestination) went a long way in falling prey to the temptation of reckoning with such an "other God." (IV/1, 181, italics added)

33. I take it that Barth is here presupposing a theme he has developed elsewhere: "The hiddennes of God is the inconceivability of the Father, the Son and the Holy Spirit, of the one true God, . . . who as such is known only to himself, and is therefore viewable and conceivable only to himself, and alone capable of speaking of himself aright, i.e., in truth" (II/1, 197).

When it comes to God's relationship with the world, Barth argues, we cannot abstract from God's pretemporal decision of election. "We have to do with [God's] free but definitive decision. We cannot abstract from it without falling into arbitrary speculation" (II/2, 6). God must always be regarded as the triune God, not as "an arbitrarily conceived absolute" (II/2, 24). Speculation arises when we do "not start with the concrete biblical form of these qualities [mercy and righteousness] and of God himself [as the Holy Trinity]" (II/2, 135). Calvin would have been better off "if his understanding of predestination had been less speculative and more in accordance with the biblical testimony" (II/2, 18). The alternative to "arbitrary speculation concerning an arbitrarily conceived absolute" is in fact "the exposition of Scripture, and therefore *a testimony to the revelation of the triune God*" (II/2, 24, italics added).

The question we must consider at this point is Barth's understanding in II/2 of what counts as "speculation." Here again we have a matter on which revisionists and traditionalists disagree. Why did Barth think that Calvin's doctrine of predestination tended toward "disastrous speculation" in the doctrine of God? Why did he think Calvin's doctrine of election was "speculative"? Was it merely because Calvin seemed to posit a God beyond the pretemporal decision of election (the revisionist proposition)? Or was it not rather that Calvin's doctrine of election failed to operate adequately with a doctrine of the antecedent Trinity (the traditionalist proposition)?

Calvin's doctrine of election, as Barth saw it, can be summarized as follows. God the Father was, so to speak, the legislative branch, God the Son the executive branch, and God the Holy Spirit the judicial branch. Calvin's deep mistake was not to include the entire antecedent Trinity in the legislative branch, where the pretemporal decision of election was made. Instead, Jesus Christ became the object and executor of election. He did not belong to the legislative branch. Therefore the decision of election or predestination was not determined by him as an acting subject.[34]

34. Barth's critique of Calvin here was based mainly on a reading of Calvin's *Institutes*. He did not take Calvin's commentaries into account, which would complicate the picture. It seems that for Calvin "predestination" covers both "election" and "reprobation." Thus when he writes that "Christ makes himself the Author of election" (*Inst*. III.22.7), that does not obviate Barth's concern about a hidden God

Just as Jesus Christ was not the Subject of election, so also for Calvin he was not the object of rejection. Only God the Father decided who would be among the elect and who among the rejected. It was a decision with two separate outcomes. In the eternal decree of predestination, the Son pertained only to the outcome of election, but not to that of rejection. The elected Son was not (as in Barth) the gracious and vicarious bearer of rejection.

For Calvin, there was more to God in the "legislative branch" than became manifest through the Son in the "executive branch." Although the Son revealed that God was the Father of mercy (for the elect), nonetheless God was at the same time a God of righteousness and wrath (for the reprobate). This other, terrifying side to God did not seem to be determined by Jesus Christ. In his incarnate person, it was not something that he moderated, mediated, and contained.

What Calvin failed to grasp, for Barth, was the trinitarian nature of the "legislative branch," and most especially the essential role of Jesus Christ within it. Calvin was driven, Barth suggests, "to *speculating* about a *decretum absolutum* instead of grasping and affirming in God's electing the manifest grace of God" (II/2, 105, italics added). His view of the "legislative branch" was speculative precisely because it was insufficiently christocentric and trinitarian.

For Barth, Calvin failed to see that it was the whole Trinity (Father, Son, and Holy Spirit), not just God in abstraction, who was the Subject of election. He failed to see that "the Subject of this decision is the triune God—the Son of God no less than the Father and the Holy Spirit. And the specific object of it is the Son of God in his determination as the Son of Man, the God-Man, Jesus Christ, who is as such the eternal basis of the whole divine election" (II/2, 110).

Calvin did not see that from all eternity Jesus Christ was the one who elects and not just the one who was elected. He failed to see that pretemporal election took place in "the harmony of the triune God" (II/2, 105). He did not see that

> the obedience which he renders as the [antecedent] Son of God is, as genuine obedience, his own decision and electing, a decision and

---

of predestination whose double decree is not determined, in both aspects, by the mercy of Christ.

> electing no less *divinely free* than the electing and decision of the [antecedent] Father and the [antecedent] Holy Spirit. Even the fact that he is elected [as the Son of Man] *corresponds* as closely as possible to his own electing [as the antecedent Son]. (II/2, 105, italics added)

Calvin did not see that the freedom of divine election is the freedom of the antecedent Trinity. Calvin's doctrine of election was therefore "speculative" in Barth's eyes precisely to the extent that it was not grounded in the Trinity. It was not speculative for drawing upon that idea but precisely for neglecting it. It was speculative because it did not properly start with the "concrete biblical form" of God himself in his self-revelation as the Holy Trinity and then think about pretemporal eternity from there (II/2, 135). It was speculative, in other words, because it posited in effect a hidden God outside and beyond the Holy Trinity. Although Calvin's doctrine of the Trinity may have been impeccably orthodox in itself, he did not make proper use of it at this point. There was a hidden and terrifying God in eternity over against the revealed God of mercy and grace.

We turn now to the revisionist position. According to the revisionists, Barth could not have criticized Calvin's doctrine of election for being "speculative" while then going on himself to ground election in the antecedent Trinity. By revisionist lights, the antecedent Trinity as such was just as "speculative" as the view Barth was criticizing in Calvin. We read in the "Grace and Being" essay,

> But that God is triune *for the sake of* his revelation? How could Barth deny this [i.e., the revisionist view of the Trinity's subsequence] without positing a mode of existence in God above and prior to God's gracious election—the very thing he accused Calvin of having done? How can he (or anyone else) know that God is triune in and for himself, independent of his eternal will to be revealed? (101–2, italics added)

Note again that no claim is made here that Barth ever adopted the revisionist rejection of the antecedent Trinity or that he regarded the Trinity as being grounded in election. Rather, the claim is again a matter of deductive reasoning. Only on pain of "inconsistency," it is suggested, could Barth have posited an antecedent Trinity "above and prior to" God's pretemporal decision of election (102). If he were to have posited such a Trinity (as of course he did), his views would have been just as "abstract" and "speculative" as those he supposedly rejected in Calvin.

But of course, as should be evident by now, Barth did exactly what the revisionists would deny he did. The antecedent eternal Trinity was, in his eyes, the necessary and sufficient condition of God's trinitarian self-revelation (and by the same token also of election). As such, the antecedent Trinity was in fact not "abstract" but the *ens concretissimum*. It was not "speculative" but the essential guarantee of revelation's freedom, veracity, and reliability.

Contrary to revisionism, it was precisely *because* Barth embraced the idea of an eternally antecedent Trinity that he worried in II/2 about Calvin's "speculative" doctrine of election. Moreover, Barth could indeed uphold his view of the antecedent Trinity without lapsing into self-contradiction. Indeed, he would have been inconsistent with himself if he had not affirmed it in this regard. For the later Barth as for the earlier Barth of *Church Dogmatics*, the antecedent Trinity was neither "abstract" nor "speculative."

Furthermore, when it comes to being "abstract" and "speculative," we might wonder how Barth would have looked on the suggestion of a pre-trinitarian God beyond God. For Barth, as over against the revisionists, being essentially trinitarian was not something "discretionary" for God. It was not eternally contingent but rather eternally noncontingent (in line with traditional ecumenical theology). As will be documented below, for Barth, even in II/2, God would be the antecedent Trinity whether the world had been created or not. The revisionists reject this kind of statement as untenable, though they are willing to concede that even without creating the world God *might* have been trinitarian (but then again he might not have been).

In *Engaging the Doctrine of God*, Professor McCormack explains once more that Barth should never have spoken of God in himself "apart from and prior to the eternal act of self-determination to be God-for-us in Jesus Christ."[35] In other words, Barth should never

35. See Bruce L. McCormack, "The Actuality of God: Karl Barth in Dialogue with Open Theism," in *Engaging the Doctrine of God: Contemporary Protestant Perspectives*, ed. Bruce L. McCormack (Grand Rapids: Baker Academic, 2008), 185–244; on 215. Further page references cited in the text.

have spoken of the antecedent Trinity as existing prior to election and creation in such a way that it still would have existed without them. Perhaps not, but that's exactly what he did, even in II/2, and then continually afterward. The argument continues,

> If we think ourselves to know precisely what God would be had he not determined himself to be God-for-us in Jesus Christ [as Barth did], if we think ourselves to know how his being would have been constituted in the absence of his relation to us [again, as Barth did], then we have looked away from God's being in the act of his self-revelation [as Barth did not] and have made ourselves *guilty* of thinking on the basis of some form *of metaphysical essentialism* [again, as Barth did not]. God *might* still have been triune—though what precise form that might have taken is impossible to say. (215–16, italics added)

Several matters invite comment here. First, in a familiar move, the revisionist Barth who arises from deductive reasoning is again pitted against the actually existing textual Barth. Second, a chain of argument is introduced that leads to more non sequiturs. It does not follow that Barth's doctrine of the antecedent Trinity means that he has looked away from God's being in the act of self-revelation. Nor does it follow that Barth is guilty of thinking on the basis of metaphysical essentialism. Note the forced option again between "actualism" and "essentialism," as if there were no other possibilities. Finally, the tentative status ascribed to God's trinitarian identity is remarkable. If God had not chosen to create the world, "God *might* still have been triune," we are told, but then again he might not have been (216, italics added). Whether to be triune without the world would apparently be discretionary for God. It would seem that prior to his trinitarian self-actualization through election, God existed not as pure act but as some sort of indeterminate potency.

How would Barth have assessed the proposal that God's trinitarian identity was somehow discretionary? Would he not have regarded it as a tacit form of modalism? Did he not define modalism as involving "a Hidden Fourth" that stood behind "three mere manifestations" in the sense of its being logically and ontologically prior to them (I/1, 355, rev.)? Is not revisionism's "God beyond the Trinity" just this sort of Hidden Fourth? Doesn't it threaten to make the economic Trinity into something "foreign to [God's] essence" (I/1, 382)?

How is it that there could be a prior and unheard of Divine Reality with the power to "give himself being" by "constituting" himself as the Trinity (though allegedly he lacks any "essence")? Does not this strangely indeterminate Ultimate Reality threaten to make God's revelation into something "bounded as it were above and within, so that we have to ask about the Hidden Fourth if we are really to ask about God" (I/1, 382, rev.)? Is not this prior Divine Reality by definition "a neutral, undifferentiated Fourth" (I/1, 396, rev.)? Does it not seem to threaten "the dissolution of [God's] triunity" into something logically and ontologically more basic (I/1, 396)?

Above all, isn't revisionism's "God who gives himself being" the very essence of "abstraction" and "speculation"? Does it not posit a Deity who *might* not be trinitarian if there were no election or incarnation? "Will not the question of the hidden God emerge one day as the question of the true God"—outside and beyond the Trinity (II/2, 66)? Regarding this anonymous Divine Entity, are we not faced with a *Deus nudus absconditus*? If so, are we not compelled to object that this strange Entity is not "the *Deus revelatus* who is as such the *Deus absconditus*, the eternal God," but rather a hidden God who stands outside and prior to the revealed God (II/2, 111)? What reason could we possibly have to posit an indeterminate Deity prior to the Trinity? How could this untenable proposal claim for its warrant a logically more "consistent" Barth?

2

Seek God Where He May Be Found

An Important Exchange

After "Grace and Being," the next important essay in the controversy would be Professor McCormack's "Seek God Where He May Be Found: A Response to Edwin Chr. van Driel."[1] The initial piece by Professor van Driel was published along with Professor McCormack's response.[2] The van Driel/McCormack exchange affords us an opportunity to discuss matters deferred until now.

Using the Principle of Charity

A definite virtue of the van Driel essay is that it honors the principle of charity. Professor van Driel does not proceed as though Barth's idea

1. Bruce McCormack, "Seek God Where He May Be Found: A Response to Edwin Chr. van Driel," *Scottish Journal of Theology* 60 (2007): 62–79. (Henceforth references to this essay are cited by page number in the text.)

2. Edwin Chr. van Driel, "Karl Barth on the Eternal Existence of Jesus Christ," *Scottish Journal of Theology* 60 (2007): 45–61. (Henceforth references to this essay are cited by page number in the text.)

that "Jesus Christ is the Subject of election" is so unambiguous that only one way to interpret it exists. For him the statement is difficult to understand. Without mentioning the charity principle, Professor van Driel looks at four possible interpretations in order to find one that might relieve Barth of his supposed "inconsistency." This is the principle of charity in action.

The first two interpretations may be dealt with rather quickly. As Professor van Driel presents them, they are mirror images of each other. The one thinks that Barth's view of eternity overpowers his view of history as the place where Christ enacts our salvation. The other starts from Christ's historical work of salvation and argues that Barth's view of eternity merely reflects on it. The one worries when it finds Barth making baffling statements that the incarnation is somehow eternal. The other appeals to Barth's view that what is sequential for us in time is present all at once in eternity. Professor van Driel rejects the first view, associated with Emil Brunner and G. C. Berkouwer, because it fails to see that for Barth divine revelation does not pertain to things rigidly determined. The second one, associated with John Colwell, does not account, Professor van Driel thinks, for Christ's presence in eternity as the Subject of election.[3]

A third view, Professor's McCormack's revisionism, receives more attention. Professor van Driel wonders (as I have here) how God can constitute himself by giving himself being. He concludes that "the notion of divine self-constitution is incoherent" (56). He goes on to argue that if election constitutes the divine being, then creation must also be necessary for God to be God. "If election is an essential act of God," reasons Professor van Driel, "so is the incarnation. But incarnation implies creation: it implies humanity" (54). Further, if creation is constitutive of divine being, then it seems that Hegel might be lurking in the background. "I do not see," writes Professor van Driel, "how [Professor] McCormack would end up at a different place than Hegel, even if his starting point—will rather than nature—is different" (54). In short, Professor van Driel rejects Barth-revisionism largely on analytical grounds. At the same time, however, he also argues (as I have) that it does not comport with the actually existing textual Barth (51–53, 58–60).

3. I myself find more promise in the second approach, as will be seen.

What then are we to make of Barth's assertion that "Jesus Christ is the Subject of election"? Because it lies at the heart of the revisionist/traditionalist controversy, this assertion needs to be examined carefully. It needs to be interpreted, furthermore, in a nonrevisionist manner if the traditionalist position is to succeed. Does Professor van Driel help us here? Unfortunately it seems that he does not. While his argument is clever, it is perhaps finally too clever by half.

What we need is an account of how Jesus Christ can be the acting Subject in God's pretemporal decision of election. What Professor van Driel gives us, however, is an ingenious but finally immaterial account of how, for Barth, Jesus Christ is not the acting Subject of election but instead "the verb, the action" (58). "The name 'Jesus Christ,'" we are told, "picks out, not a subject, but an act and determination of divine willing" (58). For Barth, according to Professor van Driel, it is God who is the acting Subject in election through his self-determination as Jesus Christ. Although this line of reasoning is on the right track, it does not entail that Jesus Christ is, in and of himself, the Subject of election. In other words, Professor van Driel explains the problem by explaining it away.

Recall what is stipulated by the principle of charity. If a plausible interpretation can be constructed that saves Barth from the charge of incoherence, it is to be preferred to one that tries to hoist him with his own petard. It is not a question of whether Barth's assertion is enigmatic. It is precisely that. The first point to see, therefore, is that contrary to revisionism, its interpretation is not self-evident. Its proper interpretation cannot be achieved merely through deductive reasoning.

It must not be forgotten that Barth is trying to understand the New Testament. He did not invent the idea that before the world was created Jesus Christ was somehow present in eternity. It is written that he was loved by the Father "before the foundation of the world" (John 17:24). It was also "before the foundation of the world" that he is said to have been "foreknown" by God as the one who would die like a spotless lamb on the cross (1 Pet. 1:20). In a similar way he is described even more astonishingly as the Lamb "slain from before the foundation of the world" (Rev. 13:8 KJV). It is also written that "before the foundation of the world" we were "chosen" in him (Eph. 1:4), a clear reference to pretemporal election.

Furthermore, it is Jesus Christ (not the Logos *asarkos*) who is said to have played a role in the work of creation: "One Lord, Jesus Christ, through whom are all things and through whom we exist" (1 Cor. 8:6). "For by [our Lord Jesus Christ] all things were created, in heaven and on earth, visible and invisible, whether thrones or dominions or rulers or authorities—all things were created through him and for him" (Col. 1:16). "He was"—Barth takes this passage as referring to the Word made flesh—"in the beginning with God. All things were made through him, and without him was not any thing made that was made" (John 1:2–3). "From him and through him and to him are all things" (Rom. 11:36). According to the clear witness of the New Testament, Jesus Christ is believed to have been present in the beginning with God. He is thought somehow to have existed in eternity before the foundation of the world. The question is, in what sense?

Three points can help us to grasp the way in which this mystery was interpreted by Barth.

God Has Indeed No Beginning

First, for Barth, the Holy Trinity has no beginning, "for God has indeed no beginning" (II/2, 102). (This is an important clue about how Barth uses the word *beginning*.) Therefore, to say that Jesus Christ was present "in the beginning" does not make him into a constitutive member of the Trinity (as the Logos *ensarkos*), for his humanity obviously has a beginning. It is therefore not the Logos *ensarkos* as such who is eternally begotten of the Father but rather (as in all traditional ecumenical theology) the Logos *asarkos*. Nor is the Logos begotten merely for the sake of becoming *ensarkos*, as if God had no subsistence in and for himself.

There is no Godhead—no divine *ousia*—that is not already that of the Holy Trinity. "There is no such thing as Godhead in itself. Godhead is always the Godhead of the Father, the Son and the Holy Spirit" (II/2, 115). There is therefore no "pre-trinitarian" Divine Entity who morphs into the Holy Trinity through God's pretemporal decision of election. On the contrary, the divine decision of election is a decision of the antecedent Trinity—"the decision of the Father, Son and Holy Spirit" (II/2, 105).

It is the Holy Trinity (which has no beginning) that is operative in the pretemporal decision of election. The Trinity is therefore operative "in the beginning," which for Barth means at the beginning of all God's ways and works with the world, at the beginning of his *decretum et opus ad extra* (his decree and work as directed externally toward the world). Election presupposes the Trinity, because it is the Trinity that effects pretemporal election. In election the antecedent Trinity determines itself to deal graciously with the world. (All this is said in II/2.) Barth writes,

> In the beginning, before time and space as we know them, before creation, before there was any reality distinct from God which could be the object of the love of God or the setting for his acts of freedom, God anticipated and determined within himself (in the power of his love and freedom, of his knowing and willing) that the goal and meaning of all his dealings with the as yet non-existent universe should be the fact that in his Son he would be gracious towards man, uniting himself with him. (II/2, 101)

Before the universe existed God determined himself to be God for us, but he did not thereby "constitute" himself as Father, Son, and Holy Spirit, for the simple reason that he was already perfectly constituted as the Holy Trinity in and of himself at the beginning of all things. "In the beginning it was the choice of the Father himself to establish this covenant with man by giving up his Son for him, that he himself might become man in the fulfillment of his grace" (II/2, 101).

I would interpret this statement as follows. At the beginning of all things, the antecedent Father (who has no beginning) chooses to give up his antecedent Son (the Logos *asarkos*, who also has no beginning) in order to establish his covenant with humankind. The antecedent Father, in other words, elects that his antecedent Son might become human for the sake of the world. God chooses that the Logos *asarkos* might become the Logos *ensarkos* in the fulfillment of his grace. Barth continues. "In the beginning it was the choice of the Son to be obedient to grace, and therefore to offer up himself and to become man in order that this covenant might be made a reality" (II/2, 101).

I interpret this statement along the same lines. Likewise, at the beginning of all things, the antecedent Son (who has no beginning) chooses obedience to the antecedent Father (who also has no beginning) for the sake of grace toward the as yet nonexistent universe. He, the Logos *asarkos*, chooses to offer himself up and become human, to become the Logos *ensarkos*, in order that the divine covenant of grace might become a reality. Barth concludes this trinitarian account:

> In the beginning it was the resolve of the Holy Spirit that the unity of God, of Father and Son, should not be disturbed or rent by this covenant with man, but that it should be made the more glorious—the deity of God, the divinity of his love and freedom, being *confirmed and demonstrated* [*bestätigen und bewähren*] by this offering of the Father and this self-offering of the Son. (II/2, 101–2, rev.; italics added)

Again, my (somewhat belabored) interpretation would be as follows. The antecedent Holy Spirit (who has no beginning) was also present at the beginning with the antecedent Father and the antecedent Son. How could it be otherwise? It was the resolve of the antecedent Spirit—the eternal Spirit of peace—that the oneness of the antecedent Father and Son should not be disturbed or torn apart by the covenant of grace with the as yet nonexistent human creature, even though this covenant would mean the death of the incarnate Son (the Logos *ensarkos*) on the cross. The love and freedom of the triune God would be "confirmed and demonstrated" (not "constituted") by this covenant of grace. In this covenant the oneness of the antecedent Father and the antecedent Son would be made "the more glorious." In it they would not give themselves being (*per impossible*) but would rather glorify their eternal and always existent being (*ousia*) (which has no beginning). The antecedent oneness of their eternal being as it subsisted "in the beginning" would be made all the more glorious in the Spirit by this offering of the antecedent Father and this self-offering of the antecedent Son. Barth concludes,

> This choice was in the beginning. As the subject and object of this choice, Jesus Christ was at the beginning. He was not at the beginning of God, for God has indeed no beginning. But he was at the beginning of all things, at the beginning of God's dealings with the reality which is distinct from himself. Jesus Christ was the choice or election of God in respect of this reality. He was the election of God's grace

> as directed towards man. He was the election of God's covenant with man. (II/2, 102)

Barth's discourse here shifts from speaking about "the Son" to speaking about "Jesus Christ." Jesus Christ—whose humanity is not antecedent and eternal, but contingent and temporal—now enters the picture. He was at the beginning of all God's ways and works with the as yet nonexistent creation. Note what is explicitly stated: "He was not at the beginning of God, for God has indeed no beginning" (II/2, 102). Jesus Christ was not at the "beginning" of God (who has no beginning), but rather at the beginning of all God's ways and works with the world.

Revisionism seems to claim that God indeed has a "beginning," at least in his trinitarian identity. It suggests that Jesus Christ was at the beginning by which God "constituted" himself through pretemporal election. This idea is not borne out by the material that we have just read from II/2.

It must not be overlooked, however, that Barth adds, "As the subject and object of this choice, Jesus Christ was at the beginning" (II/2, 102). If "this choice" was entirely the choice of the antecedent Trinity, as I have argued, how is it possible that Jesus Christ can now be described not only as its "object" but also as its "subject"? How can he have been present "at the beginning" in such a way that he participates in—indeed that he constitutes—God's pretemporal decision of election? How is it that Jesus Christ himself subjectively determines all God's ways and works with his creation "from before the foundation of the world"? These questions form the very nub of the controversy between the revisionists and the traditionalists. If the traditionalists cannot provide a satisfactory answer at this point, their argument is in trouble.

God's Eternity as the Conjunction of Simultaneity and Sequence

For Barth, the mystery of Jesus Christ's presence at the beginning of all things belongs to the larger mystery of God's eternity. Two false pictures can be ruled out at once. The first would be that the eternal Son who is operative at the beginning is simply the Logos *asarkos*. It is not simply the Logos *asarkos* in himself and as such who is said to be present at the beginning. To that extent the revisionists are correct. The second, however, would be that the Jesus Christ who is present at the beginning (as the Logos *ensarkos*) is pre-existent in the same sense as God (who has no beginning) is pre-existent. The incarnate Son (the Logos *incarnandus/incarnatus*) is obviously not present at the "beginning" of the triune God, but rather at the beginning of God's relation to the world. To that extent the traditionalists are correct.

For Barth, Jesus Christ is present at the beginning in his identity as the eternal Son of God who elects to become the temporal Son of Man. The term *Jesus Christ* is defined as "the Son of God in his oneness with the Son of Man, as foreordained from all eternity" (II/2, 104). As the elected man, Jesus Christ is principally the electing God. In the decision of election, "he (as God) wills himself (as man)" (II/2, 117). In other words, as the antecedent Logos *asarkos*, he wills himself as the subsequent Logos *ensarkos*. It is obviously not the Trinity that is subsequent to the incarnation, but the incarnation that is subsequent to the Trinity.

Apart from election, we know God's will "only as the act in which from all eternity and in all eternity, God affirms and confirms himself [as the Trinity]" (II/2, 155). "We must guard against disputing," Barth warns, "the eternal will of [the triune] God which precedes even predestination. We must not allow God to be submerged in his relationship to the universe or think of him as tied in himself to the universe" (II/2, 155). Here Barth is clearly at variance with the revisionists.[4]

4. Barth's statement that God's eternal will "precedes" predestination (II/2, 155) does not, as Matthias Gockel claims, "squarely contradict" what Barth states elsewhere when he says that the election of Jesus Christ is "God's eternal will" (II/2, 146). Dr. Gockel does not take into account that for Barth the phrase "God's eternal will" can be used in more than one sense. The divine $will_1$ that precedes predestination, in which God is fully the triune God in and of himself, is the presupposition of the divine $will_2$ by which God determines himself to be for the world in election. (These are two aspects of one and the same divine will.) What God is and wills in himself is the presupposition of what God is and wills by grace. Again, these are not two different divine wills, but one and the same will in two aspects. (The first aspect is noncontingent while the second is non-necessary.) Like other revisionists, Dr. Gockel fails to see that God's eternal will is intrinsically differentiated and complex. Although he accuses Barth of contradiction, he makes no effort to apply the

Divine election, according to Barth, is an eternal event with historical ramifications. "When we speak of the divine predestination," he writes, "we speak of an eternal happening" (II/2, 184). Election takes place in eternity "before and above all things and all events" (II/2, 183). It is a "once for all event" that takes place "eternally before time" and therefore "above time" and "beyond time" (II/2, 183). As the "election of Jesus Christ," however, this event is not merely eternal. "Notwithstanding its eternity, it is history. It stands in the midst of all history. It is one history with other histories. It is the self-attestation of eternity" (II/2, 160).

To borrow language used by Barth in a slightly different connection, the election of Jesus Christ, as it takes place at the beginning of all things, "points to an eternal happening and to a temporal: to an eternal in the form of time, and to a temporal with the content of eternity" (II/2, 97). It has, so to speak, a complex double location. "It occurs in the very midst of time no less than in that far distant pre-temporal eternity" (II/2, 184). "As the content of eternity before time [existed], it cannot remain beyond time. *Per se* [in itself] it is in time as well as before time" (II/2, 188). "From all eternity God elected to bear this name. . . . Jesus Christ is the eternal will of God, the eternal decree of God and the eternal beginning of God" relative to the as yet uncreated world (II/2, 99). Barth sums up:

> We can and must say that Jesus Christ was in the beginning with God in the sense that all creation and its history was in God's plan and decree with God. But he was so not merely in that way. He was also in the beginning with God as "the first-born of every creature" (Col. 1:15), himself the plan and decree of God, himself the divine decision with respect to all creation and its history, whose content is already determined. Everything that is embraced and signified in God's election of grace as his movement towards the human creature, everything that results from that election and everything that is presupposed in such results—all these are determined and conditioned by the fact that that election is the divine decision whose content is already determined, that Jesus Christ is the divine election of grace. (II/2, 104, rev.)

principle of charity, another revisionist shortcoming. See Matthias Gockel, *Barth and Schleiermacher on the Doctrine of Election* (New York: Oxford University Press, 2006), 178.

As a composite divine-human reality, Jesus Christ enjoys an unprecedented eternal-historical location. He necessarily belongs to history, but not only to history. He also belongs essentially to eternity as the eternal divine Word (Logos *asarkos*) who elects to become one with a particular human being (Logos *ensarkos*), namely, with the historical man Jesus. As the eternal divine Word who elected to become flesh for the sake of the world, Jesus Christ belongs to the complex dynamics of eternity without any detriment to his full and genuine historicity. He is the eternal God in the form of time and a historical human being with the content of eternity. He stands in the midst of history in connection with all other histories as eternity's presence and self-attestation. He is therefore historical but not merely historical, because he is also and primarily eternal. He transcends time even as he partakes of it, and he partakes of time even while eternally transcending it. This is the mystery of Jesus Christ, the eternal Word made flesh, as confessed by faith.

For Barth, the cross of Christ, the last judgment, and God's pretemporal decision of election are (from one perspective, *sub specie aeternitatis*) not three different events but three different forms of one and the same event (cf. II/2, 60). They are three moments of one and the same divine act (cf. III/2, 497). They remain eternally distinct while also coinhering. They coinhere eternally in a dynamic and perichoretic fashion. As three distinct forms of a single indivisible event, they mutually contain, anticipate, recapitulate, ground, and fulfill one another (cf. IV/3, 296). As Barth says in a closely related connection, "They are mutually related as forms of this one action by the fact that each of them contains the other two by way of anticipation and recapitulation, so that without losing their individuality or destroying that of the others, they participate and are active and revealed in them" (IV/3, 296). Without losing their threeness, these three—the cross, the last judgment, and pretemporal election—are one.

For Barth, there are "temporal" distinctions in God's eternity but no "separations."

> That being is eternal in whose duration beginning, succession, and end are not three but one, not separate as a first, a second and a third occasion, but one simultaneous occasion as beginning, middle and

> end. Eternity is the simultaneity of beginning, middle, and end, and to that extent it is pure duration. Eternity is God in the sense in which in himself as well as in all things God is simultaneous, i.e., beginning and middle as well as end, without separation, distance or contradiction. (II/1, 608, rev.)

Jesus Christ is present at the beginning of all things because he is made to participate in the dynamics of the divine eternity. "God's 'before' and 'after,'" Barth suggests, "are not separated from one another" (II/1, 623). "God's eternity is in time. Time itself is in eternity." And Jesus Christ himself is the One who absolutely determines both time and eternity (without "constituting" them) (II/1, 623).[5] "In [God's eternal] present there occurs both the beginning and the end. At God's end, his beginning is operative in all its power, and his present is still present. At this point, as in the doctrine of the Trinity itself, we can and must speak of a *perichoresis*, a mutual indwelling and interworking of the three forms of eternity" (II/1, 640).

As God's pretemporal decision of election, Jesus Christ enjoys a unique place by grace in both time and eternity, and therefore at the beginning of all things. He is made to exist at the beginning as the One he will be in time. He is present in the eternal foreknowledge and counsel of God. "It is not that God knows everything because it is, but that it is because [God] knows it" (II/1, 559). Jesus Christ is the subject and object of election in eternity because that is how he is known by God. He is present at the beginning because God foreknows, elects, and appoints him to be the One in whom all things are determined by grace. "Everything that God knows he also wills, and everything that he wills he also knows" (II/1, 551). "Everything that exists outside [God] does so because it exists first and eternally in [God], in his knowledge" (II/1, 559). This prior and eternal mode of existence in God is enjoyed supremely by Jesus Christ because he is foreknown, elected, and appointed to be the actualization of grace to all things. "But as this creature—because this is what God sees and wills—he is before all things, *even before the dawn of his own time* [*auch vor dem Anbruch seiner eigenen Zeit*]" (IV/2, 33, original emphasis restored).

5. For Barth something can be "determined" (or modified) only if it has already been "constituted."

As previously noted, Barth asserts that the Word had "already" taken upon himself our human nature "in the eternal sight of God" (III/1, 54). Barth points to "the counsel of God from all eternity and before creation" according to which "Jesus, the Christ, and therefore very God and very man" already exists concretely as such in pretemporal eternity (III/1, 51). This form of his existence is presupposed in pretemporal election.

The idea of God's eternal foresight and counsel entails that the presence of Jesus Christ "in the beginning" is not merely virtual but real. He is present even in his humanity as the one whom God knows eternally as the object of election. On this basis, as will be explained, he is also present as the Subject of election.

Because everything that exists outside God exists first of all in God, in his eternal sight or foreknowledge, it follows "that [God's] knowledge is not actually tied to the distinction between past, present, and future being" (II/1, 559). It is again supremely the person of Jesus Christ in his irreducible historicity who, for God, *sub specie aeternitatis*, is not tied to the distinction between past, present, and future being. Supremely, although along with all else, he is "foreknown by God from all eternity, or, to put it in temporal terms, [he is known] always—no less and no differently in [his] future than in [his as yet nonexistent historical] present and past" (II/1, 559, rev.). Jesus Christ, the Word made flesh, exists "in the beginning" with God, because he is foreknown, elected, and appointed from all eternity to be the actuality of grace for the world.

In short, because of his complex double location, the presence of Jesus Christ "in the beginning" may be described as at once "virtual" and yet also "real." Insofar as the incarnation is not yet "actualized in the manger of Bethlehem, the cross of Calvary and the tomb of Joseph of Arimathea" (III/1, 51), his existence in the eternal foreknowledge and counsel of God is in some sense "virtual." He is truly present to God in principle and in essence but not yet directly in his historical actualization.

However, insofar as Jesus Christ is indeed present in the eternal foreknowledge and counsel of God, his presence is real and not just virtual. Whatever is real to God in his eternal foreknowledge and counsel is unequivocally real, not just hypothetically or potentially.

Jesus Christ is present "in the beginning" with God as "an eternal [event] in the form of time, and [as] a temporal [event] with the content of eternity" (II/2, 97). In the beginning, he is no less real to God in pretemporal eternity than he will be in time, and as he is real in God's pretemporal foreknowledge and counsel, so he will also be actualized in time. "From him and through him and to him are all things" (Rom. 11:36).

Logos Asarkos *and Logos* Ensarkos*: How Are They Related?*

The man Jesus is not the Son of God by nature. "He is the Son of God only by the grace of God" (II/2, 121). "The man Jesus as such has nothing to bring before the electing God which would make him worthy of the divine election or make his election necessary" (II/2, 121). Although in some sense he belongs to the Holy Trinity, he does so not by nature but by grace, not by eternal generation but by historical (and thus contingent) participation. As a historical human being, the man Jesus is assumed by grace into union with the eternally antecedent Son. "In [Jesus Christ] it comes to pass for the first time that God wills and posits another being different from himself, his creature" (II/2, 121). As the union of the eternal Son with the man Jesus, Jesus Christ is the One from whom, through whom, and to whom are all things (Rom. 11:36).

But God did not need this union with him to establish his triune identity. He did not need it in order to "constitute" himself. On the contrary, he was already fully constituted in and of himself. In II/2 Barth repeatedly affirms that the Trinity is prior to election.

> Be it noted that this determination of the will of God, this content of predestination, is already grace, for God did not stand in need of any particular ways or works *ad extra*. He had no need of a creation. *He might well have been satisfied with the inner glory of his threefold being, his freedom, and his love.* (II/2, 121, italics added)

> From all eternity God could have excluded man from this covenant. He could have delivered him up to himself and allowed him to fall. He could have refused to will him at all. He could have avoided the compromising of his [divine] freedom by not willing to create him. *He*

> *could have remained satisfied with himself and with the impassible glory and blessedness of his own inner [trinitarian] life.* But he did not do so. He elected man as a covenant-partner. In his Son he elected himself as the covenant-partner of man. (II/2, 166, italics added)

> In this primal decision God did not remain satisfied with his own [triune] being in himself. He reached out to something beyond, willing something *more than his own being*. He willed and posited the beginning of all things with himself. But this decision can mean only an *overflowing* of his glory. *It can consist only in a revelation and communication of the good which God has and also is in himself [as the Holy Trinity]. If this were not so, God would not be God.* (II/2, 168–69, italics added)

These key passages from II/2—which state clearly that God could have remained satisfied with the inner glory of his threefold being—show clearly that he did not need to constitute himself in relation to the world. Even in II/2 Barth never posited a God who *might* have been the Holy Trinity but rather spoke of a God who would never under any circumstances have been anything else. For Barth God's trinitarian identity was irreducible, primordial, and definitive. As in all standard ecumenical theology, it was unconditioned and absolute. It was not indeterminate in itself but intrinsically glorious, impassible, and complete. God might well have been completely satisfied with it—with "the inner glory of his threefold being" (II/1, 121). He did not need to create and redeem the world. Nor was his triune being a consequence of election. He was self-sufficient as the Holy Trinity in and for himself.

As I have documented extensively elsewhere, statements like those just cited are found over a span of more than three decades: from 1932, when Barth first began the *Church Dogmatics*, up until 1968, the year he died.[6] These statements strongly disconfirm the central revisionist contention. What is significant here is that we find them even in II/2, the volume where, for Barth, election was supposed to constitute the Trinity. But clearly the reverse is true. For Barth, election presupposes the Trinity, and it is the Trinity that constitutes election.

6. See George Hunsinger, "Election and the Trinity: Twenty-Five Theses on the Theology of Karl Barth," *Modern Theology* 24 (2008): 179–98; on 181–82.

> The fact that [God] is not satisfied, but that *his inner [trinitarian] glory overflows and becomes outward*, the fact that he wills the creation, and the man Jesus as the first-born of all creation, is grace, sovereign grace, a condescension inconceivably tender. But this determination of the will of God is eminently grace to the extent that in relation to this other, the creation of God, God's first thought and decree consists in the fact that in his Son he makes the being of this other his own being, that he allows the Son of Man Jesus to be called and actually to be his own Son. (II/2, 121, italics added)

In his eternal Son—in the antecedent, fully determinate Logos *asarkos*—God makes the being of this other, namely, the man Jesus, his own. "He *allows* the Son of Man Jesus to be called and actually to be his own Son" (II/2, 121, italics added). He allows this union to take place—by grace alone. Again, God does not need it by nature in order to establish his triune identity. He is already the triune God in full glory without it.

> In and with his lordship over this other, in and with the creaturely autonomy of this other—and even that is grace—God wills and decrees and posits in the beginning both his own fatherhood [*ad extra*] and also the sonship of the creature. This is more than mere kindness and condescension. It is self-giving. And that is how *the inner [trinitarian] glory of God overflows*. From all eternity it purports and wills its own impartation to the creature, the closest possible union with it, a fellowship which is *not to its own advantage* but to that of the creature. It is in being gracious in this way that God *sets forth* his own glory. It is in the election of the man Jesus that his decision to be gracious is made. (II/2, 121, italics added)

Election represents the free overflowing of the superabundant glory of the triune God. It is a matter of sheer excess, not a matter of God actualizing a mere potency or filling up an inner deficit. What can the election of all others in Jesus Christ be if not grace? What can it be "but more grace, a participation in the One [Jesus Christ] who elects, a participation in his creatureliness (which is already grace), and a participation in his sonship (which is eminently grace)" (II/2, 121)? The grace of election is therefore "*the overflowing of God's inner glory*" (II/2, 122, italics added). It is the "decisive act of history, . . .

the actualization of the overflowing of the inner glory of God" (II/2, 125–26).

> God's glory overflows in this the supreme act of his freedom. . . . The [antecedent] Son of God determined to give himself from all eternity. With the Father and the Holy Spirit, he chose to unite himself with the lost Son of Man. This Son of Man was from all eternity the object of *the election of Father, Son, and Holy Spirit*. And the reality of this eternal being together of God and man is a concrete decree. It has as its content one name and one person. This decree is Jesus Christ, and for this very reason it cannot be a *decretum absolutum*. (II/2, 158, italics added)

Election can only mean sheer grace: the overflowing, the revealing, and the communicating of God's prior trinitarian glory.

> Our starting-point must always be that in all his willing and choosing, what God ultimately wills is himself. All God's willing is primarily *a determination of the love of the Father and the Son in the fellowship of the Holy Ghost*. How, then, can its content be . . . anything else but glory—a glory which is new and distinctive and divine? But in this primal decision God does not choose only himself. In this choice of self he also chooses another, that other which is man. Man is the outward cause and object of this overflowing of the divine glory. (II/2, 168-69, italics added)

In this overflowing of his intrinsic inner glory, the triune God does not become the living God, because in and of himself he is already the living God. "God does not . . . become the living God when he works or decides to work *ad extra*—in his being *ad extra* he is, of course, the living God in a different way—but his being and activity *ad extra* is merely an overflowing of his inward activity and being, of the inward vitality which he has in himself" (II/2, 175).

Election is therefore the "overflowing of God's inward being as the living God" (II/2, 176). In this overflowing, the life of God's own inward freedom and love is in no way "limited or questioned but rather confirmed" as what it eternally is (II/2, 176). God's glorious inward being is not established by election but expressed in a new and different way.

> What else can we say when the elect Son of Man is God's own Son, God himself in his own self-giving? The One elected [the Son of Man] testifies unequivocally to the nature and being of the One who elects [the Son of God]. He [the Son of Man] speaks for that One [the Son of God]: a posteriori, of course; and only in virtue of the fact that that One first speaks for him, that the Son of Man is taken up into union with the [antecedent] Son of God. The Son of Man speaks, in fact, for the grace of God which stoops down to man and lifts up man to itself. He speaks not for himself but for the mercy of God. (II/2, 176)

In this connection Barth explicitly warns against "absolutizing" God's pretemporal decision of election. The pretemporal decision would be absolutized if it were regarded as constituting rather than expressing God's inmost trinitarian reality. Barth cautions,

> We must resist the temptation to absolutize in some degree the concept of choosing or electing. We must not interpret the freedom, the mystery and the righteousness of the election of grace merely as the definitions and attributes of a supreme form of electing posited as absolute. We must not find in this supreme form as such the reality of God. (II/2, 25)

We must not mistake election as the supreme form of God's freedom, mystery, and righteousness, as if God were not already supremely free, mysterious, and righteous in himself as the antecedent eternal Trinity. Election means that the eternal Son is sent to enter into union with the human Jesus for the sake of the world. Election is "a spontaneous *opus internum ad extra* of *the trinitarian God*" (II/2, 25, italics added). For Barth, election presupposes (but does not constitute) the Holy Trinity, even though it represents a radical self-determination on the part of the Trinity. Election represents the spontaneous self-determination of the trinitarian God. That is why it is pure grace. Election always has "in [the triune] God himself . . . the character of grace" (II/2, 25). "Its freedom is indeed divine and therefore absolute. It is not, however, an abstract freedom as such"—as it would be if it were wrested from its eternal trinitarian location.

> We must not seek the ground of this election anywhere but in the love of [the triune] God, in his free love—otherwise it would not be his—but

> still in his love. If we seek it elsewhere, then we are no longer talking about this election. We are no longer talking about the decision of the divine will which was fulfilled in Jesus Christ. We are looking beyond these to a supposedly greater depth in God. (II/2, 25)

In short, "the Subject of this decision is the *triune* God. . . . And the specific object of it is the Son of God [in his freely chosen union with the Son of Man] . . . who [the triune God in and through the Son] is *as such the eternal basis of the whole divine election*" (II/2, 110, italics added).[7] Or again, "In the primal and basic decision in which he wills to be and actually is God, in the mystery of what takes place from and to all eternity within himself—*within his triune being*—God is none other than the One who in his Son or Word elects himself, and in and with himself elects his people" (II/2, 76, rev.; italics added).

For Barth, "the election of the man Jesus as such" rests upon "the election and personal electing of the Son of God *which precedes* [*vorangeht*] *this election*" (of Jesus) (II/2, 107, italics added). In other words, the eternal Son's being elected (by the Father) and his personal electing of himself are prior (logically and ontologically) to the electing of the man Jesus, because the eternal reality of the Trinity is presupposed by election and precedes it. All these statements from II/2 run contrary to Barth-revisionism.

We may now return to the question of the divine Logos. What status does it have in relation to election and therefore to the incarnation? The matter can be clarified as follows.

The incarnation testifies to the eternal Word. The Logos *ensarkos*, the Son of Man in union with the Son of God, testifies to the nature and being of the Logos *asarkos*, the prior and eternal divine Son, who elects him (the Son of Man), and prior to doing so also elects and determines himself. The Logos *ensarkos* (the Son of Man in union with the eternal Son) speaks for the Logos *asarkos* (the eternal Son) but only after the fact (a posteriori), only in virtue of the fact that he (the elected Son of Man) is taken up into union with the prior and eternal divine Son (through pretemporal election) so as to form one person with him as the Word made flesh. More simply, the Logos

7. In this statement Barth is expressing his agreement with the view of Athanasius.

ensarkos is constituted when the Logos *asarkos* elects the man Jesus and assumes him into union with himself.

Therefore, the relationship of the Logos *ensarkos* to the Logos *asarkos* is not one of dialectical identity (as it seems to be in the revisionist proposal). The Logos *ensarkos* and the Logos *asarkos* are not related to one another like Wittgenstein's duck/rabbit or like the faces/vase image in a figure/ground illustration. They do not form a single self-identical reality that can be looked at in two different ways. They do not compose a figure with two aspects such that when looked at in one way it appears as the Logos *ensarkos* while when looked at in another it appears as the Logos *asarkos*, as if the two were dialectically one and the same without remainder.

Nor does the Logos *asarkos* simply disappear into the Logos *ensarkos*, as if the former were merely a preliminary stage on the way to the latter. The Logos *asarkos* is not exhausted in its secondary form as the Logos *incarnandus/incarnatus/ensarkos*. It is not like a moth-worm that eventually morphs into a moth, or a child that develops into an adult. The Logos *asarkos* in itself and as such is not preliminary but antecedent, not transitory but eternal, not provisional but perpetual and enduring.

It might be mentioned at this point that in II/2 Barth articulates a completely traditional understanding of the Logos *asarkos*. "The Word as such is before and above all created realities. It stands completely outside the series of created things. It precedes [*vorangeht*] all being and all time. It is like God himself. As was rightly said concerning it in the expositions of the 4th century: 'There was no time when it was not'" (II/2, 95, rev.).

The "Word as such," the Word that "stands completely outside the series of created things," the Word that precedes "all being and all time," is obviously the Logos *asarkos*. It is this Word as the eternal Son that enters spontaneously into union with the Son of Man (Jesus of Nazareth) to form the Logos *ensarkos* at the beginning of all things, from before the foundation of the world.

The relationship of the Logos *asarkos* to the Logos *ensarkos* may therefore be described as one of asymmetrical unity-in-distinction. It is a matter of one eternal divine Logos acting in two different forms. The two forms are indivisibly one. By free divine grace there is no

Logos *asarkos* that is not *also* the Logos *ensarkos*, and no Logos *ensarkos* that does not presuppose its *ground* in the Logos *asarkos*. The two forms of the one divine Logos coexist and indeed coinhere simultaneously, without either of them losing its distinctive identity. They coexist and coinhere dynamically in a single divine action that is inwardly differentiated and complex.

In their dynamic interrelations, the two forms of the one Logos remain abidingly distinct. In particular, as already noted, the Logos *asarkos* does not disappear into the Logos *ensarkos* without remainder, either by way of self-transformation or of dialectical identity. For Barth, the Logos *asarkos* continues to be operative, as we have seen, in a way that is concealed and incomprehensible to us, within the inner divine life of the Holy Trinity (IV/1, 52).

> [The man Jesus] is to the created world, and therefore *ad extra*, what the Son of God as the eternal Logos is within the triune being of God. If the eternal Logos is the Word in which God speaks with himself, thinks himself and is conscious of himself, then in its identity with the man Jesus it is the Word in which God thinks the cosmos, speaks with the cosmos and imparts to the cosmos the consciousness of its God. (III/2, 147)

> In this free act of the election of grace there is already present, and presumed, and assumed into unity with his own existence as God, the existence of the man whom he intends and loves from the very first and in whom he intends and loves all other men, of the man in whom he wills to bind himself with all other men and all other men with himself. In this free act of the election of grace, the Son of the Father is no longer *just* [*bloß*] the eternal Logos, but as such [*als solcher*], as very God from all eternity, he is also [*zugleich schon*] the very God and very man he will become in time. (IV/1, 66, original italics restored)

The dynamic relationship between these two forms of the one divine Logos is not only one of unity-in-distinction. It is also asymmetrical and therefore irreversible. The Logos *asarkos* is irreversibly antecedent even as the Logos *ensarkos* is irreversibly subsequent. The one indivisible Logos is simultaneously *asarkos* by nature and *ensarkos* by grace. Its primary form as *asarkos* is the logical and ontological ground of its secondary form as *ensarkos*. Likewise, its secondary form as *ensarkos* is, by grace alone, the appointed goal of its primary form as *asarkos* with respect to God's relationship with the world.

In the Word made flesh and therefore in its form as the Logos *ensarkos*, the essence of the divine Word is completely abased—even as the human essence that it has assumed is completely exalted (IV/2, 110). At the same time, in its form as the Logos *asarkos*, the eternal Word transcends this abasement even as it fully participates in it. If there were no such transcendence, there would be nothing but abasement. In that case, the human essence could not be exalted in and through the incarnate Word.[8]

Only if the incarnate Word fully participates in the flesh—in misery and death as the consequence of human sin—while still eternally transcending it at a higher level can our sin, misery, and death possibly be overcome. The humiliation of the Word may in some sense be total, but it is not for that reason exhaustive. At a higher level, the Word in its form as the Logos *asarkos* at once sustains itself in its radical abasement as the Logos *ensarkos* while still also enjoying the transcendent communion and peace that belong to it as a "person" of the eternal Trinity.[9] The actuality of the multiple and simultaneous forms of the one Word of God in its diverse temporal and eternal operations surpasses anything that we can think or imagine. That is the surpassing mystery of the divine Logos.

In short, the two forms of the one divine Logos, *asarkos* and *ensarkos*, are dynamically related by a pattern of asymmetrical priority, indissoluble unity, and abiding distinction. In its *asarkos* form, the one Word of God coinheres with all that it does in its *ensarkos* form while still eternally preceding and transcending it. In its *ensarkos* form, on the other hand, the one Word of God coinheres in its prior eternal and transcendent *asarkos* reality so that all abasement can be abolished and life can be brought forth out of death. The relationship of the Logos *ensarkos* with Jesus is indissoluble, so that the Word will never cease

8. In line with traditional Reformed theology, Barth rejects the *genus maiestaticum*. See IV/2, 71–78. For an interesting discussion, see Piotr J. Malysz, "Storming Heaven with Karl Barth? Barth's Unwitting Appropriation of the *Genus Maiestaticum* and What Lutherans Can Learn from It," *International Journal of Systematic Theology* 9 (2007): 73–92.

9. It is the role of the Holy Spirit to ensure this (II/2, 101).

to be *ensarkos* even as it simultaneously remains also in some sense *asarkos* and transcendent in ways beyond human comprehension.

As Sumner concludes in his fine study of Barth on this question,

> The lives of the Word as *asarkos* and *ensarkos* both mutually participate in the one Christ, just as his two natures (or essences) mutually participate. This, for Barth, is simply another way of speaking of the hypostatic union—but speaking of it as a dynamic event between God and humanity and not as a static condition.[10]

In the mystery of the triune God, the one eternal Son operates (variously) in both time and eternity as Logos *ensarkos* and Logos *asarkos* at the same time.

Jesus Christ as the Subject of Election

With a long account behind us, we are now in a position to explain Barth's enigmatic statement that Jesus Christ is the Subject of election.[11] A major reason why Barth insists that Jesus Christ is the Subject of election is that he wants to rectify a problem in the tradition. He wants to overcome the view—found in virtually all medieval and Reformation sources—that posits Jesus Christ as merely the object of election. For Barth, Jesus Christ is not merely its object nor can he be relegated (as with Calvin) merely to the "executive" branch. As the second "person" of the Trinity, the eternal Son (in union with Jesus of Nazareth) belongs (with the Father and the Holy Spirit) to the "legislative" branch in God's pretemporal decision of election.

"In [Jesus Christ]," writes Barth, "we have to do not merely with elected man but with the electing God" (II/2, 108). Jesus Christ is the electing God and the elected man in one. "The name of Jesus Christ has within itself the double reference: the One called by this name is both very God and very man. Thus the simplest form of the dogma may be divided at once into the two assertions that Jesus Christ is

10. Sumner, "Twofold Life of the Word," 15 (n31 in chap. 1 above).

11. In this section I have revised and corrected some of the views expressed in my essay "Election and the Trinity" (*supra* n6).

the electing God, and that he is also elected man" (II/2, 103). In the mystery of his one divine-human reality, Jesus Christ is the Subject of election as God and the object of election as man.

Barth enters an important clarification:

> We have laid down and developed two statements concerning the election of Jesus Christ. The first is that Jesus Christ is the electing God. This statement answers the question of the Subject of the eternal election of grace. And the second is that Jesus Christ is elected man. This statement answers the question of the object of the eternal election of grace. Strictly speaking, the whole dogma of predestination is contained in these two statements. (II/2, 145)

Jesus Christ is the Subject of election in an internally differentiated way. He is its Subject not only as God but also as man, but first and primarily as God. "As we have to do with Jesus Christ," writes Barth, "we have to do with the electing God" (II/2, 54). Or again, "Jesus Christ . . . in his own person is himself the God who freely elects and then acts towards the creature, the One behind and above whom there is no other God and no other election. . . . Christ is the electing God" (II/2, 68). The tradition was right to see that the man Jesus is the object of election but wrong to forget that by virtue of the hypostatic union he is also and primarily the electing God.

Jesus Christ is the electing God in his person as the eternal Son. But precisely as the eternal Son (prescinding from his elected humanity), he is not only the one who elects but also the one who is elected. In and with his election of the man Jesus, the eternal Son elects himself. From all eternity, he elects himself as the one who is elected by the Father. He is therefore not only executor but also legislator of the eternal divine decree.

> The eternal Son is elected, ordained, and sent by the Father to be its executor. But if he and the Father are one in this unity of the divine name and glory, a unity in which there can be no question of rivalry, then it is clear that the Son, too, is an active Subject of the *aeterna Dei praedestinatio* as Son of Man, that he is himself the electing God, and that only in this way, and therefore in an unlimited divine sovereignty, is he the Elect, the One who is subjected to the divine predestination,

> the Son who is voluntarily obedient to the Father; that only in this way and for this reason is he the Son of Man establishing and fulfilling the will of God in the world. (II/2, 107)

The eternal Son who is elected by the Father also elects himself. In unity with the Father, he is an active Subject of the eternal predestination of God (*aeterna Dei praedestinatio*). He is the electing God along with the Father. But what does he elect? "God does not first elect and determine man but himself" (IV/2, 84). The eternal Son first elects himself as the basis of all God's ways and works with the world.[12]

Let us look at this event more fully. In electing himself, the eternal Son also elects Jesus of Nazareth. He elects him, that is, in order to assume him into union with himself. Note, however, that the eternal Son's election of himself is said to precede (logically and ontologically) his election of Jesus. As we have noted earlier, for Barth "the election and personal electing of the Son of God . . . precedes [*vorangeht*] . . . the election of the man Jesus as such" (II/2, 107, rev.). In and with electing himself, the eternal Son of God also elects himself as the Son of Man. As Barth states in a slightly different connection, in electing himself, the eternal Son "has united himself with the man Jesus of Nazareth, and in him and through him with this people" (II/2, 8). The election of Jesus of Nazareth in and with the self-election of the eternal Son is what makes the whole God-Man Jesus Christ present as such (proleptically) at the eternal beginning of all things.

The idea of "prolepsis" helps to explain how the New Testament can speak about the God-Man Jesus Christ as present with God "before the foundation of the world." The word *prolepsis* means "anticipatory realization" as opposed to simply "real anticipation." Through the coinherence of simultaneity and sequence in eternity, Jesus Christ, truly God and truly human, is present at the beginning of all things. He is conceived as present by virtue of God's eternal foreknowledge, in which something is true and real because it is divinely foreknown (not the reverse).

Note especially that the idea here in Barth is *prolepsis*, not *incarnandus*. The claim at this point is not merely that the eternal Son is

12. We leave to one side here Barth's doctrine that when the eternal Son elects himself, he elects to be rejected for our sakes and in our place.

ordained to become incarnate in time. The claim is rather the more radical one that in the mind of God the earthly Jesus is already present as such to the eternal Son and assumed into hypostatic union with him in pretemporal eternity. Jesus Christ is also present by virtue of God's eternal will, according to which he is the object of pretemporal election. His election, as we have seen, enjoys a double temporal location: it occurs before time as well as in time (though in different respects) (II/2, 184). It occurs in both simultaneity and sequence. "From all eternity God elected to bear this name" (II/2, 99). In the eyes of God, the whole God-Man Jesus Christ already exists concretely before the foundation of the world (III/1, 51). He is present in pretemporal eternity because the eternal Son, in and with electing himself, has willed and elected to make himself one with Jesus of Nazareth. In and through the decision of the electing Son, Jesus is present before he exists as "the man who was in the beginning with God." He is present as "the man who was marked and sought out by God's love." He is present as "the man to whom and to the existence of whom the whole work of God applied as it was predetermined from all eternity" (II/2, 180).[13]

An especially important passage regarding this prolepsis appears in IV/1.

> [God] will not restrict himself to the wealth of his perfections and his own inner life as Father, Son, and Holy Spirit. In this free act of the election of grace there is already present, and presumed, and assumed into unity with his own existence as God, the existence of the man whom he intends and loves from the very first and in whom he intends and loves all other human beings, of the man in whom he wills to bind himself with all other human beings and in whom all other human beings will be bound with himself. In this free act of the election of grace, the Son of the Father is no longer **just** the eternal Logos, but as such, as very God from all eternity he is also the very God **and** very man he will become in time. (IV/1, 66, rev., original boldface restored)

In God's free election of grace, what is the relationship between the man Jesus and the eternal Trinity, and in particular between Jesus

13. This would be my version of the "Colwell solution" that is rejected by Professor van Driel, as noted in n3 above.

and the eternal Logos? Barth's answer in this passage is as follows. God's own inner life as Father, Son, and Holy Spirit subsists in "the wealth of his perfections." God could have remained satisfied with these perfections because his inner life lacks nothing in itself (II/2, 121; IV/1, 213, etc.). Nevertheless, the triune God will not restrict himself to the wealth of his inner life. In his free act of election, he posits that which is outside himself (*opus internum ad extra*). The triune God does not just posit the creation in general. He posits the man Jesus as the object of election. In and through the election of this one particular man, all other human beings (and indeed the whole cosmos) will be bound to God and God to them. In the pretemporal election of grace, the man Jesus is "intended and loved" from the very first, and all others are "intended and loved" in him.

In pretemporal eternity, the man Jesus is already "present" and "presumed" through a kind of prolepsis. He is already "assumed into unity" with God's own existence as the triune God. In particular he is assumed into unity with the eternal Son. The Son is and remains who and what he is as the eternal Logos, that is, as the Logos *asarkos*. But he is no longer *merely* the Logos *asarkos*. "*As such*, as very God from all eternity, he is *also* the very God and very man he will become in time" (IV/1, 66, italics added).

> For in the eternal election of God he [the man Jesus] is, along with God's Son, the first, i.e., the primary object and content of the primal and basic will of God. He is not, of course, a second God. He is not eternal as God is. He is only the creature of God—bound to time, limited in other ways too. . . . But as this creature—*because this is what God sees and wills*—he is before all things, *even before the dawn of his own time*. As the primary object and content of the creative will of God he is in his own way just as really in the presence of God and with God as God is [to himself in his own reality]. He [this man], too, has a basic reality *in the counsel of God* which is the basis of all reality. At no level or time can we have to do with God without having also to do with this man. . . . But he was and is there first, the one whom God has elected and willed, who is there in being. (IV/2, 33, rev.; italics added)

In concert with the entire Trinity, the eternal Son elects the man Jesus into personal (hypostatic) union with himself. Without ceasing to be the Logos *asarkos*, "but as such," the Logos is now "also" not only very God but very man as well (IV/1, 66). In pretemporal eternity, the eternal Logos is already (proleptically) the incarnate Son that he will become in time. The man Jesus is not only the object of election, but as such he is also the object of the *assumptio carnis*. The man Jesus is already "intended" (*meint*). He is "already present, and presumed, and assumed" (proleptically) (*schon gegenwärtig, schon vorweggenommen, schon hineingenommen*) into unity with the eternal Son (IV/1, 66). The eternal Son, who elects Jesus of Nazareth, will then become in time what he already is in eternity. He will actualize himself in time as the incarnate Son. The eternal Son is in this sense the Subject of election.

Finally, "the Son . . . is an active Subject of the *aeterna Dei praedestinatio* as Son of Man" (II/2, 107). Not only does the eternal Son elect the man Jesus as the object of election, and not only does the Son elect himself in accord with his being elected by the Father, but he is also an active Subject of pretemporal election as the Son of Man. I take this to mean that in being the object of divine election, the human Jesus also consents to it at the same time. Although he is the object of election, he is not merely a passive object. He actively receives his election and consents to it. Although his human will is abidingly distinct from the eternal Son's divine will, the two are of one accord. They coexist and coinhere in an asymmetrical pattern of unity-in-distinction. In the eternal predestination of God, these two wills—the divine and the human—cooperate in perfect harmony by virtue of the hypostatic union.

At the same time, moreover, Jesus as the elected human being consents to his election through his own electing of God. "The one who is elected from all eternity can and does elect God in return" (II/2, 178). In other words, he not only consents to his being the object of election but also reciprocates by affirming and electing the One who elected him.

In sum, we have the following complex transaction: (1) the eternal Son is elected by the Father, (2) the eternal Son elects himself in consent to the Father, (3) in electing himself the eternal Son elects the man Jesus into indissoluble unity with himself, (4) the man Jesus elects himself by consenting to be the object of divine election, and finally (5) the man Jesus consents to his election by electing the God who elected him. All this is conceived as one indivisible but internally differentiated event, and, remarkably, all this is conceived as occurring (initially) in pretemporal eternity. In this pretemporal occurrence the man Jesus is conceived as being present in being with the Holy Trinity proleptically according to the eternal counsel, foresight, will, and intention of God.

To be clear, Barth should not be mistaken as teaching a pretemporal incarnation. There is only one incarnation, and it takes place only as Christ is "conceived by the Holy Ghost and born of the Virgin Mary." But as such, Barth posits, the incarnate Son has a proleptic *form* in pretemporal eternity, according to God's eternal foreknowledge and will, that determines the beginning of all God's ways and works with the world.

Note yet again that this whole complex transaction presupposes the eternal Trinity in its antecedent reality.

> The Son of God determined to give himself from all eternity. With the Father and the Holy Spirit, he chose to unite himself with the lost Son of Man. This Son of Man was from all eternity the object of the election of Father, Son and Holy Spirit. (II/2, 158)

> On the one hand there is the acting Subject, God himself in his mode of existence as the Son, who is of one divine essence with the Father and the Holy Spirit. And on the other hand there is human essence, to which the Son of God gives (his own) existence and actuality, no longer being *only* [*nur*] the Son of God in this act, but becoming and being *also* [*auch*] the Son of Man. (IV/2, 84, italics added)

> It is true that he does not elect alone, but in the company of the Father and the Holy Spirit. . . . In the harmony of the triune God, he [Jesus Christ] is no less the original Subject of this electing than he is its original object. And only in this harmony can he then also [*dann auch*] be its object, i.e., completely fulfill not his own will but the will of the Father, and thus confirm and to some extent repeat as elected man the election of God. This all rests on the fact that from the very first he [Jesus Christ] participates in the divine election; that that election is also his election; that it is he himself who posits this beginning of all things; that it is he himself who executes the decision which issues in the establishment of the covenant between God and man; that he too, with the Father and the Holy Spirit, is the electing God. (II/2, 105, rev.)

> [The triune] God does not, therefore, become the living God when he works or decides to work *ad extra*—in his being *ad extra* he is, of course, the living God in a different way—but his being and activity *ad extra* is merely an overflowing of his inward activity and being, of the inward vitality which he has in himself. . . . We cannot assert too strongly that in the election of grace it is a matter of the decision and initiative of the divine good-pleasure, that as the One who elects, God has *absolute precedence* over the one who is elected. (II/2, 175, 177, rev.; italics added)

There can be no doubt that for Barth Jesus Christ is the Subject of election, but (contrary to Barth-revisionism) only within a prior trinitarian context. "The Subject of this decision is the triune God—the Son of God no less than the Father and the Holy Spirit" (II/2, 110). God does not become the Holy Trinity by virtue of pretemporal election. Otherwise, among other things, his precedence as the triune God—including the already constituted eternal Son—would not involve "the absolute precedence of God" [*des schlechthinigen Vorranges Gottes*] (i.e., antecedence) over the man who is elected (II/2, 177).

> From all eternity [*schon in Gottes ewiger Vorherbestimmung*: already within God's eternal prior determination], God is within himself the living God. The fact that God is means that from all eternity [*von Ewigkeit her*] God is active in his inner relationships [*inneren Beziehungen*] as Father, Son, and Holy Spirit, that he wills himself and knows of himself, that he loves, that he makes use of his sovereign freedom, and in doing so maintains and demonstrates [not constitutes] himself. (II/2, 175)

> In the inner life of God, as the eternal essence of Father, Son and Holy Ghost, the divine essence does not, of course, need any actualization. On the contrary, it is the creative ground of all other, i.e., all creaturely actualizations. Even as the divine essence of the Son, it did not need his incarnation, his existence as man . . . to become actual. (IV/2, 113)

Jesus Christ indeed "participates" in the eternal divine decree also in his humanity (II/2, 105). As elected man, he can even be said in a certain sense to "repeat" the eternal election of the triune God (II/2, 105). He does so, however, only by virtue of the prior self-election of the eternal and pre-existent Son, in which the man Jesus is included by grace. It is primarily as the eternal divine Son that Jesus Christ is the Subject of election, because it is only by virtue of the eternal Son that the man Jesus—in mysterious but indissoluble union with the Son—has himself been elected to be present, proleptically, in eternity as the beginning of all God's ways and works with the world.

I conclude once again with the statement that should have blocked Barth-revisionism at the outset: *Daß Jesus Christus der Sohn Gottes* ist, *das beruht freilich nicht auf Erwählung* (*KD* II/2, 114). "Of course, the fact that Jesus Christ *is* the Son of God does not rest on election" (II/2, 107, rev.).

Barth simply reiterates here a point he had long since made at the beginning of the *Church Dogmatics*: "Jesus Christ does not first become God's Son when he is it for us. He becomes it from eternity; he becomes it as the eternal Son of the eternal Father" (I/1, 427).

This idea is restated in volume IV.

> The Son of God does not need his humanity. . . . He does not need any completion, any concretion, any form which perhaps he lacks. He is not an abstraction. . . . Nor is he an empty *prius* ["before"] which waits to be filled out by something actual. . . . He is actual in himself—the One who is originally and properly actual. (IV/2, 53–54)

Barth's views on this question never changed. Throughout the later volumes of *Church Dogmatics*, he reaffirms, as we will continue to see, what he had been insisting all along.

> If we will not listen to the fact that Christ is antecedently God in himself in order that in this way and on this basis he may be our God, then we turn the latter, his being God for us, into a necessary attribute of God. God's being is then essentially limited and conditioned as a being revealed, i.e., as a relation of God to humankind. The human creature is thus thought of as indispensable to God. But this destroys God's freedom in the act of revelation and reconciliation, i.e., it destroys the gracious character of this act. (I/1, 420–21 rev.)[14]

14. This remark represents a central worry of the traditonalists about Barth-revisionism.

If the claim is that II/2 represents a sea change in Barth's dogmatics because he drastically reversed the order of Trinity and election, then a careful examination shows that the claim will not bear scrutiny. Although Barth's views continued to develop in the course of the *Church Dogmatics*—sometimes in surprising ways—there is no fundamental break between II/1 and II/2.

Conclusion

In conclusion, the differences between Professor van Driel and Professor McCormack may be revisited. If it is correct to say that in pretemporal election the Son of God and the Son of Man already operate in terms of the hypostatic union—in a Chalcedonian pattern of asymmetrical unity-in-distinction—then each of these scholars gets only half the picture. Whereas Professor van Driel gets the distinction without the unity, Professor McCormack gets the unity without the distinction.

Professor van Driel, in effect, grasps the role of the antecedent divine Son but only at the expense of his proleptic unity with the earthly Son of Man.[15] He fails to see that the role of the Son of Man is intrinsic, not extrinsic, to the role of the eternal Son. The earthly Son of Man is not merely the passive object of election. Although he repeats the decision of pretemporal election and makes it his own, he does so without separation or division in pretemporal eternity from the eternal Son.

From the standpoint of eternity (*sub specie aeternitatis*), the Son of Man is already present in the beginning as a secondary but real electing subject. He is present proleptically in hypostatic union with the eternal Son. Already in pretemporal eternity, the will of the earthly Son of Man (as a human subject) is enhypostatic and anhypostatic with that of the eternal Son (as a divine Subject). At the beginning of all things, the eternal Son of God as election's primary Subject is never without the Son of Man as election's object and secondary subject. The two wills in Jesus Christ, creaturely and divine, are already indissolubly

15. Although Professor van Driel sees Jesus Christ as an event more than as election's acting Subject, his emphasis falls on God as the acting Subject in abstraction from what Barth calls "the Son of Man."

one by virtue of their (proleptic) hypostatic union. From before the foundation of the world, in the eyes of God (and therefore in reality) they operate together inseparably in a pattern of asymmetrical unity-in-distinction.

Professor McCormack, on the other hand, grasps the earthly Son of Man in his indissoluble unity with the eternal Son, but only at the expense of their abiding distinction. Whereas Professor van Driel tends in effect toward christological dualism, Professor McCormack tends toward christological monism. He tends to conflate the earthly Son of Man with the eternal divine Son, who is thought to become "determinate" only in the decision of election. Relative to the earthly Son of Man, the eternal divine Son has no antecedent, determinate reality in eternity. Jesus Christ is presented as the Subject of election only from the standpoint of his (earthly) divine-human unity. The distinction between his (logically and ontologically prior) divine will and his human will is blurred and confused.

Barth's rejection of monothelitism should not be neglected here. In line with the Sixth Ecumenical Council, Barth upheld the abiding distinction in Jesus Christ between his human and divine wills, although his human will was never independent of his divine will (I/2, 158). "The early Church knew what it was doing," he wrote, "in the monothelite controversy when it distinguished and juxtaposed the divine and human wills in the person of Jesus" (II/2, 605, rev.). Having removed the idea of Jesus Christ as the Subject of election from its rich (antecedent) trinitarian context, Professor McCormack not only treats this idea as an abstract proposition from which erroneous deductions can be drawn but also underestimates the Chalcedonian complexity inherent in the God-Man Jesus Christ as an acting Subject. In particular, he fails to do justice to the (fully constituted) antecedent eternal divine Son as election's primary Subject and object.

These tendencies toward either christological dualism or christological monism, respectively, are more implicit than explicit. They pertain to the Barth interpretations of these two scholars, not necessarily to their own christological views. What both interpretations miss, however, is Barth's highly distinctive idea.

Barth posits that Chalcedonian Christology involves an astonishing pretemporal aspect. He uses it to make sense of New Testament passages where Jesus Christ is said to exist as such "before the foundation of the world." He assumes that the hypostatic union cannot be absent from the pretemporal decision of election.

The idea of "Jesus Christ as the Subject of election" is therefore to be explained as follows. In the far reaches of pretemporal eternity, the God-Man Jesus Christ is the Subject of election, along with the Father and the Holy Spirit, in his full divine-human unity and therefore in his two wills, which coexist (and coinhere) proleptically in a mysterious pattern of asymmetrical unity-in-distinction. By virtue of his election and his union with the eternal Son and therefore by virtue of the eternal foreknowledge and counsel of the triune God, the man Jesus is present in pretemporal eternity, before the dawn of his own time, as the one he will be in time. He is present in this sense before the foundation of the world. But the God-Man Jesus Christ is also the Subject of election within time insofar as he ratifies in time what took place in eternity. He is thus election's Subject, for Barth, in both a pretemporal and a supra-temporal (or "in-temporal") sense (cf. II/1, 623)—and not the one without the other.[16]

One last point of clarification. In saying that "Jesus Christ is the Subject of election," Barth wants to say that God's decision of election involves a pretemporal form of the hypostatic union. There is a union of the two "natures," and therefore of the two wills, in Jesus Christ as the eternal Son elects to unite the human essence of Jesus to himself. The eternal Son gives his own existence and actuality "to this human essence," so that he is "no longer . . . only [*nur*] the Son of God in this act, but [becomes and is] also [*auch*] the Son of Man" (IV/2, 84 rev.).

Therefore, even in pretemporal election the human essence and will of Jesus are "enhypostatic" with the divine "person" of the eternal Son (proleptically). By the same token, the essence and will of "Jesus" are also "anhypostatic." There is no "hypostasis" of Jesus qua Jesus. The only relevant hypostasis here is that of the divine Son. Jesus qua Jesus has no other hypostasis than this one. It is not a matter of two electing "subjects" or "persons" (Jesus and the eternal Son) somehow

16. Pretemporal election could then be thought of under the rubric of *opus perfectus* (perfect work), while its temporal ratification would be an *actus perpetuus* (perpetual operation). See I/1, 427.

operating alongside one another in concert. There is only one electing Subject—only one "person" or *hypostasis*—namely, the eternal Son, who in this decision makes himself really but contingently (and irreversibly) identical with Jesus of Nazareth. In this (enhypostatic) sense, it can therefore be said that already in pretemporal eternity "Jesus Christ is the Subject of election" (cf. I/2, 163).[17]

17. I would like to thank Matthew Baker for helping me to clarify this point.

Interlude

It remains for us to examine some recent developments in the revisionist camp. The characteristic features of Barth-revisionism, as we have seen them so far, are at least threefold:

1. a rationalistically deduced picture of Barth derived from abstract propositions;
2. a penchant for accusing Barth of self-contradiction without recourse to testing this perception by applying the principle of charity; and
3. a black-and-white mode of thinking that quickly narrows the options as if there were no complexities and no shades of gray.

Underlying these characteristics is a further tendency to brush aside contrary textual evidence coupled with a failure to read Barth carefully at crucial points. Barth-revisionism can be very impressive in its knowledge of Barth on the one hand while resorting to incautious assertions on the other. The distortion factor can be high.

Some younger Barth scholars, to whom we now turn, have aligned themselves with Barth-revisionism. It seems that the appeal of an "actualistic ontology" can be strong. It offers the perceived advantage of embracing a "thoroughly modern Barth" without the supposed encumbrances of "classical metaphysics" and "substance ontology."

3

Being in Action

The Question of God's Historicity

One important younger scholar who has adopted the revisionist viewpoint is Professor Paul T. Nimmo. In many ways his book on Barth's ethics, *Being in Action: The Theological Shape of Barth's Ethical Vision*, is admirable.[1] Professor Nimmo displays a remarkable command of his theme while offering a very thorough inventory of the secondary literature. He sifts through the field of Barth interpreters with a keen eye, judiciously correcting and commending them by turns. (I myself am grateful to him for pinpointing some areas where I may have been overhasty in my judgments.)

Nevertheless, dominating Professor Nimmo's book as a whole is the artificial construct of an "actualistic ontology." For him Barth's actualism is "far more than a motif" (7). In other words, it is not just an aspect of Barth's thought. It is rather a systematic construct, "an actualistic frame of reference" (6). While his language can be ambiguous, Professor Nimmo clearly leans toward reading Barth's

1. Paul T. Nimmo, *Being in Action: The Theological Shape of Barth's Ethical Vision* (London: T&T Clark, 2007). Hereafter references to this work will appear by page number in the text.

actualism as a form of "ontology$_1$" (as opposed to the more modest "ontology$_2$"). He presents Barth's entire ethics as dominated by a particular philosophical structure. "Actualistic ontology" becomes the controlling idea within which Barth works out his ethics.

Professor Nimmo can even elevate "actualism" to the point where he claims that it is "attested by Scripture" (11). He tells us that "the function of Scripture in theological ethics" is to bear "witness" to a "theological and moral ontology" (40). Barth of course argued tirelessly that the object of the biblical witness is Jesus Christ. It would seem that for Barth-revisionism matters have reached the point where an "actualistic ontology" is attested alongside him.

Professor Nimmo proceeds to display his revisionist credentials by advancing the forced option we have come to expect. We are required to choose between an "actualistic" and a "substantialistic" ontology (10n). As usual, there is no in-between. The possibility that Barth's actualism actually included "substantialistic" elements is not entertained. Barth thinks, we are told, "in an actualistic and not a substantialistic way" (89).

On this basis we are offered a view of what it means to be a person. Apparently like all "persons," God is not complete in and of himself "apart from and prior to" the "decisions, acts, and relations" that comprise his "lived existence," which seems to mean his existence in relation to the world (cf. 10n). The possibility is omitted that act and being are equally basic in God, and that God's triune "being" in and for himself is just as fundamental as the "act" in which he eternally lives in his trinitarian relations. Also ruled out is the ecumenically normative idea that God is already complete in and for himself apart from and prior (logically and ontologically prior) to his relationship with the world. The neglected options are arguably the ones that the Barth of *Church Dogmatics* actually held.

For Professor Nimmo, God cannot be self-sufficient in himself to all eternity because "election is constitutive of the being of God" (8). In support of this doubtful proposition, he quotes Barth as follows. "Everything which comes from God takes place 'in Jesus Christ,' i.e., in the establishment of the covenant which . . . God has instituted . . . between himself and his people" (II/2, 8). In Christ this covenantal commitment is "a relation in which God is self-determined, so that the determination belongs no less to him than all that he is in and for himself" (II/2, 7). Unfortunately, these statements do not support the idea that election is "constitutive" of God's being.

They actually support the traditionalist view. They support the idea that "all that God is [antecedently] in and for himself" is determined in and through Christ to be shared with the world. It is not God who is constituted by the covenant but the covenant that is constituted by God. God does not need to be "constituted," because God is already God (for Barth) in supreme glory prior to determining himself for this covenant. As Barth states again and again in II/2 (as we have seen), God's self-determination is an "overflowing" of his glory, not the filling up of some deficit as though without election God would be less than fully constituted as God. What Barth is actually saying here is that God's self-determination to be for the world "belongs no less to him" than all that he already is in himself (and in absolute self-sufficiency) to all eternity.

Professor Nimmo displays a typical Barth-revisionist error here. He confuses the idea of God's "self-determination" with that of God's "self-constitution."[2] This confusion is evident in the following remarks.

> In this actualistic ontology, then, the action of God in electing to be God for humanity in Jesus Christ is not the act of an already existing agent. Rather it is an act in the course of which God determines the very being of God. . . . There is for Barth "no state, no mode of being or existence above and prior to this eternal act of self-determination as substantialistic thinking would lead us to believe." (8)[3]
>
> If, then, God has determined to become human in the history of Jesus Christ, and if that determination is constitutive of the eternal being of

2. The revisionists oddly seem to suppose that for Barth the idea of God's "self-determination" means that God goes from an indeterminate state to a determinate state. That may be one reason why they blur it with the idea of "self-constitution." For Barth, however, self-determination means that the triune God decides to be who he is also in another and contingent way. The transition is not from the indeterminate to the determinate, but from the noncontingent to the contingent. In an act of free self-determination, contingent "properties" are added by the incarnation to God's already determinate reality as the eternal Trinity.

3. Quoting Bruce L. McCormack, "The Ontological Presuppositions of Barth's Doctrine of the Atonement," in *The Glory of the Atonement*, ed. Charles E. Hill and Frank A. James III (Downers Grove, IL: InterVarsity, 2004), 346–66; on 359. Implicit here is the erroneous claim that an ontologically prior Trinity is merely "substantialistic."

> God, then the being of God cannot a posteriori rightly be conceived without that history.[4] . . . "History could not possibly have a greater significance if even the being of God is constituted eternally, in and for itself, by way of anticipation of that which God will undergo as human in time." (108)[5]

There are a number of missteps in these statements. I will try to sort them out one by one.

- It is erroneous to say that for Barth God's pretemporal decision of election is "not the act of an already existing agent." It has been shown at some length above that for Barth "the Subject of this decision is the [already existing] triune God—the Son of God no less than the Father and the Holy Spirit" (II/2, 110). Moreover, it is not easy to see how there could be an "act" without "an already existing agent."
- It is also erroneous to say that for Barth God becomes the Holy Trinity for the sake of election. As shown above, Barth states repeatedly (even in II/2) that God is already constituted as the Holy Trinity and would remain so even without his pretemporal decision of election.[6]
- For Barth it is true that in his pretemporal act of election, God "determines" himself in a particular way, but it is not true that by this action God "constitutes" himself. For Barth, the triune God does not (and does not need to) give formal existence to himself via election.
- It is erroneous to say that for Barth there is in God "no state, no mode of being or existence above and prior to this eternal

4. Note the deductive reasoning in this statement.

5. Quoting Bruce L. McCormack, "*Justitia Aliena*: Karl Barth in Conversation with the Evangelical Doctrine of Imputed Righteousness," in *Justification in Perspective: Historical Developments and Contemporary Challenges* (Grand Rapids: Baker Academic, 2006), 167–96; on 192. God's eternal constitution is here thought to be simply an anticipation of God's relations with the world.

6. "Be it noted that this determination of the will of God, this content of predestination, is already grace, for God did not stand in need of any particular ways or works *ad extra*. He had no need of a creation. He might well have been satisfied with the inner glory of his threefold being, his freedom, and his love" (II/2, 121).

act of self-determination." It is also incorrect that the contrary proposition would commit Barth to "substantialistic thinking."

- For Barth there is indeed a reality of God "above and prior to this eternal act of self-determination." The name for this reality is "the immanent Trinity."[7]
- For Barth the idea of an immanent, antecedent, and eternal Trinity does not entail "substantialistic thinking" in any crude sense for two reasons. First, unlike revisionism, Barth does not restrict the idea of divine action only to God's relationship with the world. Second, as will be shown more fully below, he does not think that his actualism eliminates all substantialistic elements (e.g., eternality, aseity, immutability, impassibility, simplicity, etc.) from his doctrine of God.
- For Barth the act in which God has his trinitarian being in and for himself to all eternity is logically and ontologically basic. The triune God's determination of himself in the act of election, however, is logically and ontologically contingent.
- The name "Barth" in the revisionist statements above does not refer to the actually existing textual Barth. It refers, rather, to the rationalistically deduced Barth. Only the deduced Barth teaches that there is no Trinity prior to election.

• It is erroneous to say that for Barth God's act of self-determination in election is "constitutive" of his eternal being. Here we encounter one of revisionism's distinctive confusions. The word *determine* gets mixed up with the word *constitute*.

7. No one has made this point more powerfully than Paul D. Molnar. Beginning with a major book and then continuing in several distinguished articles, Professor Molnar has definitively drawn attention to the significance of the immanent Trinity in Barth. See especially Molnar, *Divine Freedom and the Doctrine of the Immanent Trinity: In Dialogue with Karl Barth and Contemporary Theology* (London: T&T Clark, 2002); Molnar, "Can the Electing God Be God without Us?," *Neue Zeitschrift für Systematische Theologie* 49 (2007): 199–222; Molnar, "Can Jesus' Divinity Be Recognized as 'Definitive, Authentic and Essential' if It Is Grounded in Election?," *Neue Zeitschrift für Systematische Theologie* 52 (2010): 40–81; Molnar, "Orthodox and Modern: Just How Modern Was Barth's Later Theology?," *Theology Today* 67 (2010): 51–56; Molnar, "Was Barth a Pro-Nicene Theologian? Reflections on *Nicaea and Its Legacy*," *Scottish Journal of Theology* 64 (2011): 347–59.

  - For Barth, to say that God "determines" himself in election means that God ordains himself to be for the creature what he already is in and for himself: the triune God who loves in freedom.
  - To put it technically, in election the triune God delimits himself by adding a differentia. He gives himself a new commitment that formally distinguishes his essence relative to what it was (logically and ontologically) before.
  - In election the triune God's essence is not constituted but presupposed, not constructed but adapted to a new circumstance. A new focus (toward the creature) is graciously added while God's eternal perfection remains the same.
  - In pretemporal election God (as the already existing eternal Trinity) determines himself, wholeheartedly and sacrificially, to be God for the fallen and otherwise lost creature.[8]
  - Election is that which makes God what he is for us but not that which makes God what he is as the triune God in and for himself.
- For Barth it would be a half-truth to assert that "the being of God cannot *a posteriori* rightly be conceived without that history." *De facto* the statement is correct. *De iure* it is incorrect, as Barth never ceases to insist by affirming (from 1932 to 1968) that the triune God would be who and what he is without the world.
- Finally, for the actually existing textual Barth, it is mistaken to assert that God needs the world to be fully realized as God, that is, to claim that "the being of God is constituted eternally,

8. The word *determine* in Barth may owe something to Kant and Hegel, who use the term in much the same way, meaning "to shape or qualify something," "to give specification to something," or "to orient something toward particular circumstances or to a particular goal." This usage can also be found in Schleiermacher and other nineteenth-century German-language theologians. It is distinct from the idea of "to constitute" in the sense of "to give something formal existence." The more subtle idea that God constitutes himself as the Trinity by virtue of determining himself for election also bears no relation to the actually existing textual Barth, as if some pretrinitarian "Divine Reality" were to morph itself into the Trinity in order to carry out the purposes of election.

in and for itself, by way of anticipation of that which God will undergo as human in time."

Relative to the actual Barth this claim is not only erroneous, it is also contrary to his deepest intuitions (II/1, 301–2). For it carries with it the consequence that God's trinitarian identity is dependent on (and therefore conditioned by) God's relationship to the world. Barth's theology strongly militates against this outcome.[9] We will return to this theme in due course.

In his book *Being in Action*, Professor Nimmo makes only a minimal attempt to provide backing for his revisionist claims about Barth. This is understandable to some extent because the focus of his book lies elsewhere. In subsequent essays, however, he does attempt to offer some evidence. His arguments are telling because they show how revisionism can misread the textual Barth.

Revisionism has recently turned its attention away from II/2, seeking confirmation in later volumes of the *Church Dogmatics*.[10] For example, appeal is now made to "The Way of the Son of God into the Far Country" (IV/1, 192–210, especially 199–204). Professor Nimmo has written an essay where he argues largely from these pages. His argument will repay our attention.

Background to IV/1, 192–210

Before turning to Professor Nimmo's argument, some preliminary remarks are in order.

9. "The creature which conditions God is no longer God's creature, and the God who is conditioned by the creature is no longer God" (II/1, 580).

10. In a groundbreaking article, Keith L. Johnson has argued that the watershed volume in Barth's *Church Dogmatics* is not II/2 (as revisionism has claimed) but rather II/1. The final phase of Barth's theological development would accordingly run from 1939 (not 1942) until his death in 1968. No major break took place in II/2. Apart from that, Professor McCormack's authoritative periodization of Barth's early development would remain intact. See Johnson, "A Reappraisal of Karl Barth's Theological Development and His Dialogue with Catholicism," *International Journal of Systematic Theology* 14 (2011): 1–23; McCormack, *Karl Barth's Critically Realistic Dialectical Theology: Its Genesis and Development 1909–1936* (Oxford: Clarendon, 1995).

- First, the passage in question needs to be read as a whole (IV/1, 192–210). It will not do to lift out certain statements while disregarding the rest.[11]
- Second, this passage is noteworthy for incorporating a kind of double ending. Like Haydn's 45th Symphony, it seems to come to an end but picks up again with a surprising new twist. However, whereas Haydn's second ending has his musicians humorously departing from the orchestra one by one so that they can go home, Barth's second ending has him returning home to himself. For in this section he endorses what he had written more than three decades earlier. He openly reaffirms the doctrine of the Trinity found in I/1, the first volume of his dogmatics.

  Not surprisingly, Barth-revisionists tend to sidestep this second ending. The ending calls into question their claim that the later Barth had disowned his early work on the Trinity.
- Third, this passage cannot be understood apart from what we have called Barth's "doctrine of antecedence." Throughout his dogmatics he used it as a basic rule.

> But we have consistently followed the rule, which we regard as basic, that statements about the divine modes of being antecedently in themselves cannot be different in content from those that are to be made about their reality in revelation. All our statements concerning what is called the immanent Trinity have been reached simply as confirmations or underlinings or, materially, as the indispensable premises of the economic Trinity. (I/1, 479)

Or again, "God does not do anything which *in his own way* he does not *have* and *is* not in himself [antecedently]" (II/1, 467, original italics restored). Or more simply, "What [God] is in revelation he is antecedently in himself" (I/1, 466).

For Barth God's actions in the economy are grounded in his living reality in eternity. Conversely, God's eternal reality supplies the

11. In the German original, a horizontal line marks a break in the text, indicating a new departure (omitted in the English translation). See Barth, *Kirchliche Dogmatik*, vol. IV, part 1 (Zurich: Theologische Verlag Zurich, 1953), 210. In the German edition this unit runs from 210–31.

"indispensable premises" for his economic operations. Because God's economic activities are grounded in his antecedent eternal reality, his eternal reality can be inferred from his economic activities. In turn, God's external deeds in the economy point to their prototypes in eternity. What God is in eternity serves as the ground and precondition—in effect, as the prototype—of all that he does in time.

In the lengthy section under consideration from IV/1, Barth continues to make use of his doctrine of antecedence. Once again God's external operations "cannot be different in content" from their basis in God's inner, antecedent reality. They differ in form—as time differs from eternity—but not in essential content. These two aspects of God's operations (temporal and eternal) continue to be described (as throughout Barth's dogmatics) in terms of "correspondence" (*Entsprechung*). In their correspondence, they comprise an asymmetrical unity-in-distinction. Therefore the two forms of the Trinity are not reversible, nor can they be collapsed into each other. They are not related by a pattern of dialectical identity, as previously explained.

Finally, as suggested in the previous point, this passage from IV/1 presupposes Barth's basic definitions of time and eternity. It is of particular importance in interpreting this section of IV/1 to remember that Barth conceives of God's eternity in a way that is trinitarian, dynamic, and concrete. The triune God exists in an eternity of "pure duration," and yet this pure duration includes the dynamic elements of "pre-temporality," "supra-temporality," and "post-temporality." These elements are thought to coinhere with one another dynamically in a way that is at once simultaneous and yet also sequential. They constitute God's (antecedent) history with himself while also serving as the eternal basis of God's history with the world. Barth writes,

> [The eternal God is alive in] pure duration, free from all the fleetingness and the separations of what we call time, the *nunc aeternitatis* [now of eternity] which cannot come into being or pass away, which is conditioned by no distinctions, which is not disturbed and interrupted but established and confirmed in its unity by its trinity, by the inner movement of the begetting of the Father, the being begotten of the Son and the procession of the Spirit from both.
>
> Yet in it there is order and succession. The unity is in movement. There is a before and an after. God is once and again and a third time,

> without dissolving the once-for-allness, without destroying the persons or their special relations to one another, without anything arbitrary in this relationship or the possibility of its reversal. If in this triune being and essence of God there is nothing of what we call time, this does not justify us in saying that time is simply excluded in God, or that his essence is simply a negation of time.
>
> On the contrary, the fact that God has and is himself time, and the extent to which this is so, is necessarily made clear to us in his essence as the triune God. This is his time, the absolutely real time, the form of the divine being in its triunity, the beginning and ending which do not mean the limitation of him who begins and ends, a juxtaposition which does not mean any exclusion, a movement which does not signify the passing away of anything, a succession which in itself is also beginning and end. (II/1, 615)[12]

There is in eternity an "inner movement" of God's history with himself. It belongs to his essence as the triune God. It consists (in part) in begetting, being begotten, and proceeding. God's inner divine essence is not simply the negation of time. In some ineffable manner it includes order, succession, and unity-in-movement. It includes a before and an after. Eternal history is the form of God's being in its triunity. This transcendent, antecedent eternal history constitutes "his essence as the triune God." His triune essence to all eternity is at once a pure duration and a dynamic history in and for itself. It neither comes into being nor passes away because the Trinity has no beginning and no ending.

Professor Nimmo on the Election/Trinity Debate

Despite its genuine merits, Professor Nimmo's contribution to the debate about election and the Trinity suffers from two main failings. First, as seems endemic to Barth-revisionism, it accuses Barth of self-contradiction without making any effort to test the assertion, as if it were obvious. It is not hard to provide an account, however, in which the supposed inconsistency disappears.

Second, the key passages that Professor Nimmo cites to support his case are not read accurately. Barth's important distinction between

12. I have reformatted this long quotation for easier reading.

time and eternity is not observed, his doctrine of antecedence is overlooked, and the difference between self-determination and self-constitution is confused. When these missteps are rectified, Barth's supposed inconsistency disappears. Moreover, when the adduced citations are restored to their proper context so that Barth's argument is taken as a whole, the untenability of the revisionist reading is confirmed.

Professor Nimmo sets up his own nomenclature. Traditionalism is styled as the "weak" view over against which revisionism is labeled as the "strong" one. "This choice of terms," we are assured, "should not in any way be taken to offer an assessment of the relative merits of either reading, but rather to indicate the relative perceived 'radicality' of the respective readings."[13] Why the revisionist interpretation should not therefore be called the "radical" reading is not explained, as if "radical" would equate automatically with "strong." In any case, perhaps the weakness of the "weak" view will prove to be stronger than the "strong" view of revisionism.

In his essay Professor Nimmo advances a thesis about the Holy Spirit. It need not detain us here except to make two points. First, it is proposed that we think about the Holy Spirit as the "elected God" along with Jesus Christ. An opinion is then offered: "While Barth himself does not avail himself of such a statement, it seems likely that he would offer his assent to it" (167). On the contrary, however, nothing could be more unlikely than Barth's assenting to such a statement. The main reason is that it has no exegetical basis in the New Testament. Nor does it make any doctrinal sense.

Barth's view is as follows. As the object of election, Jesus Christ consented to be not only elected but also rejected in our place. Along with the Father and the Son, the Spirit indeed plays a role in electing the Son. The Spirit resolves that "the unity of God, of Father and Son, should not be disturbed or rent" as the elected Son goes to the cross to be rejected in our place (II/2, 101). The Spirit thus has a particular role in the outworking of election.

13. Nimmo, "Barth and the Election-Trinity Debate: A Pneumatological View," in *Trinity and Election in Contemporary Theology*, ed. Michael T. Dempsey (Grand Rapids: Eerdmans, 2011), 162–81; on 163n. Hereafter page numbers to this essay are cited in the text.

The Spirit's task is to maintain in the economy what is already true in eternity: the undisturbed unity between the Father and the Son. It is hard to see how the Spirit could be the "object" of election (the "elected God") without entering into competition with the incarnate Son's unique saving work. It is the Son who is elected while the Spirit plays a vital, though auxiliary, role in the accomplishment of revelation and reconciliation. Neither the Father nor the Spirit, however, is elected to be rejected in our place.

Professor Nimmo's second proposal about the Holy Spirit is even less convincing. On the faulty premise that for Barth the eternal Son is begotten for (and only for) the sake of incarnation (in order to carry out the decree of election), a parallel proposal is developed regarding the Holy Spirit. The Spirit, it is suggested, proceeds for (and only for) the sake of establishing the church in history. No antecedent and independent trinitarian role exists for the Spirit in eternity (logically and ontologically)—no role, that is, such as the one Barth actually assigns to the Spirit of being the eternal (and antecedent) bond of peace between the Father and the Son. Supposedly like the Son, the life of the Spirit is viewed as exclusively or exhaustively world related. Because God has no antecedent inner life of his own, the Spirit has no place within it. Because God is evidently insufficient in himself not only apart from election but also apart from the church, the Spirit evidently has no purpose apart from helping to constitute God's being through the church. God the Holy Spirit's constitutive reason for existence is to be "enchurched" (178).

Although Professor Nimmo is not always wrong in what he affirms about the Spirit, he is wrong in what he denies. It is uncontroversial that for Barth the Spirit is ordained to mediate between Christ and the church. Among other things, the Spirit brings Christ to the church, and the church to Christ, for the sake of worship and mission. But for Barth, what the Spirit does in the economy has its antecedent ground in eternity. Precisely because to all eternity the Spirit is the mediator of communion between the Father and the Son, the Spirit can also perform various mediatorial (and Christ-centered) tasks within history.[14] As a

14. See Hunsinger, "The Mediator of Communion: Karl Barth's Doctrine of the Holy Spirit," in *Disruptive Grace: Studies in the Theology of Karl Barth* (Grand Rapids: Eerdmans, 2000), 148–85.

revisionist, however, Professor Nimmo wants to retain the Spirit's mediations within history while denying their proper ground in eternity. Whatever one might make of this project, it has little to do with Barth.

Professor Nimmo selects some texts that he admits support the "weak" (traditionalist) reading of Barth. In a worthy move, he picks them because they were written long after Barth's volume on election (II/2) and so pose a challenge to the "strong" (revisionist) view. He acknowledges that revisionists "need to account for them plausibly" (172). It will be enough to cite only one.

> The triune life of God . . . is the basis of his whole will and action even *ad extra* [outside himself], as the living act which he directs to us. It is the basis of his *decretum et opus ad extra* [decree and work outside himself], of the relationship which he has determined and established with a reality which is distinct from himself and endowed by him with its own very different and creaturely being. It is the basis of the election of man to covenant with himself; of the determination of the Son to become man, and therefore to fulfill this covenant; of creation; and, in conquest of the opposition and contradiction of the creature and to save it from perdition, of the atonement with its final goal of redemption to eternal life with himself. (IV/2, 345)[15]

According to this passage, "the triune life of God" is the basis of everything that God does outside himself. It is the basis of the "living act" that God directs to us. It is the basis of God's relating to us as creatures who are different from himself. It is the basis of God's electing us by grace in order to establish his covenant with us. It is the basis of the Son's determining to become human so that the covenant, despite being broken from our side, might still be fulfilled. It is the basis of the Son's atoning sacrifice by which our enmity toward God is overcome. It is the basis of what saves us from eternal death, redeeming us to eternal life with God.

All this—the whole sweep of God's ways and works with the world, from election and creation to atonement and redemption—is said in IV/2 to be based on "the triune life of God." There is nothing that God does *ad extra* that is not based on his antecedent self-sufficiency

15. I have cited this passage somewhat more fully than Professor Nimmo does.

as the Holy Trinity. And yet for Professor Nimmo it all comes to naught as the "weak" view.

The revisionists seem to believe they can retain all that is consequent in Barth while eradicating its antecedent ground. How, then, do they propose to deal "plausibly" with this passage from IV/2? What alternative is offered as the strength of the "strong" view?

In support of his view, Professor Nimmo appeals to a string of citations from IV/1, 192–210. They are supposed to show that for Barth "election logically precedes the Trinity." They also supposedly show that "the eternal act of election, as an act of self-determination, is primal, and [that] there is no triunity behind or without it" (173). If so, then the basis of all God's ways and works with the world would be election, not the antecedent life of the triune God.

This result from IV/1 would then stand in flat "contradiction" to what we just read from IV/2 and to much else besides. Again, however, no attempt is made to honor the principle of charity. No attempt is made to seek a reading of IV/1 that does not contradict IV/2. We are simply offered the usual claims that "Barth's writing on the relationship between Trinity and election was less than entirely consistent in his later years" (177) and that "Barth is not always fully consistent" (165). In other words, revisionism proposes to deal "plausibly" with IV/2 by once again invoking inconsistency. But was Barth really so inconsistent in his later years? When it comes to this important passage from IV/1, as will be shown, the "strong" view is not supported by careful reading.

A Reading of IV/1, 192–210

In this lengthy excerpt from "The Journey of the Son of God into the Far Country," Barth explains his purpose as reflecting on the doctrine of Christ's deity. Having looked at it from the standpoint of its "outer moment," he now turns to its "inner moment" (IV/1, 192). In other words, having examined the Son of God's obedience from the standpoint of its actualization in the economy (with special reference to Phil. 2:6–11) (IV/1, 164, 180–83), he turns to its inner basis in eternity.

The argument is an exercise in Barth's doctrine of antecedence. After considering the Son's obedience on earth, Barth asks about the condition for its possibility. What can be said about its antecedent ground? What is its eternal basis, if any, in the inner life of the Trinity (IV/1, 192)?

Only on the basis of revelation, Barth states, can we know who and what the eternal God is. It cannot be assumed that we already know what it means for God to be God. When we take our bearings from revelation, what it means for God to be God emerges as something that is at once mysterious and perhaps even offensive. What revelation tells us, Barth contends, is that "for God it is just as natural to be lowly as it is to be high, to be near as it is to be far, to be little as it is to be great, to be abroad as it is to be at home" (IV/1, 192). God as God is not merely exalted and aloof.

What is distinctive here in Barth is the idea that being exalted and being lowly are both intrinsic to God's eternal being. We can understand how God could be exalted in eternity but not how he could also be lowly at the same time. The idea of an intrinsic divine lowliness would seem to be not only mysterious but far-fetched.

Nevertheless, when God the Son humbles himself by taking the form of a servant, when he chooses to go into the far country, "he is not untrue to himself but genuinely true to himself, to the freedom which is that of his love" (IV/1, 193). No inner necessity compels God to humble himself in this way. "He does not have to choose to do this. He is free in relation to it" (IV/1, 193). For revisionism, however, it does seem as if God is under some kind of a compulsion, because without this very action (or something like it), God would not be fully "constituted" as God.

Nothing could be further from Barth's mind, however. He simply wants to show that the Son's earthly obedience has an eternal counterpart and ground. He wants to show that when "Christ is among us in humility" in the economy, he is acting in accord with "that which he is in himself, in the most inward depth of his Godhead." The incarnate Son does not become "another God" than the One he already is in himself. He appears among us precisely "as the One he was from all eternity and will be to all eternity" (IV/1, 193). Barth's emphasis on the eternal antecedence of the Son is entirely overlooked by the "strong" (revisionist) reading.

It is worth noting Barth's emphasis on eternity here. Throughout this passage he presupposes his basic distinction between time and eternity even when it is not the focus of attention. At decisive points, however, Barth appeals to it quite openly. It is a hallmark of Barth-revisionism, however, to blur the time/eternity distinction by interpreting Barth with a Hegelian slant, as we will see.

In the reading I offer here, the time/eternity distinction will be made explicit at points where it remains implicit. The validity of this move is confirmed by passages where eternity is dealt with explicitly. One of them has just been cited. Jesus Christ appears in the economy, Barth tells us, "as the One he was from all eternity and will be to all eternity." He does not first become who he is through his appearance in the economy. He does not become "another God" than the One he already is in himself (IV/1, 193).

The humility of Jesus, Barth suggests, is not merely an attitude. It reflects a relational pattern, indeed a veritable ordering principle, within the eternal God's triune being. Because there is already "a humility grounded in the being of God," God is free to reiterate this humility in Jesus. He reiterates it not because of an inner divine necessity but as "a free choice made in recognition of an appointed order" (IV/1, 193).

"Election," writes Barth, "includes a self-limitation and self-humiliation on the part of God" (IV/1, 170). But God's self-humiliation in election "does not consist in [the eternal Son's] ceasing to be himself [or indeed in coming to be himself] as man, but in taking it upon himself to be himself *in a way quite other than that which corresponds and belongs to his form as God*, his being equal with God" (IV/1, 180, italics added). In this act of self-humiliation, God does not (*per impossible*) constitute himself as God but rather becomes God for us (and also for himself) in a new and very different way. He remains the same God he always was but now assumes the form of self-humiliation and death, and to that extent he assumes the form of his opposite. He does so, as the eternal Son, in correspondence to that which belongs to his form as God.

Barth emphasizes that God's "self-emptying and self-humbling" (IV/1, 193) does not amount to a "self-contradiction" (IV/1, 186). When the eternal Son empties himself and humbles himself even unto death, what he does "cannot be alien to God" (IV/1, 193). The mystery of the divine nature or essence has an "inner side" that makes the Son "able and free to render obedience" on earth in this radical way (IV/1, 193). There is thus an inner (and antecedent) moment of obedience in eternity to which the outer moment in the economy corresponds.

The obedience of Jesus in the economy is an act that occurs "in the freedom of God, making use of a possibility grounded in the being of God" (IV/1, 194). It is not an act that engages an otherwise unused capacity. "He does not make just any use of the [limitless] possibilities of his divine nature, but he makes one definite use which is necessary on the basis and in fulfillment of his own decision" (IV/1, 194). It is a well-grounded act following a free decision of grace.

This obedience in the economy (the outer moment) is said to occur in "a holy and righteous freedom." "God is not a victim driven to and fro by the dialectic of his divine nature" (IV/1, 194). This "economic" obedience is not undertaken to fill up any theoretical divine void but "in virtue of the richness of his divine being" (IV/1, 194). It is not an arbitrary act because it takes place as "the divine fulfillment of a divine decree" (IV/1, 195). The Son's obedience in time presupposes the eternal richness of God's antecedent being as God.

This obedience in the economy has its basis "in [God's] divine nature and therefore in God himself" (IV/1, 195). But the idea of God's being obedient in and of himself is "a difficult and even an elusive" concept (IV/1, 195). "Obedience," writes Barth, "implies an above and a below, a *prius* [priority] and a *posterius* [posteriority], a superior along with a junior and subordinate. Obedience as a possibility and actuality in God himself seems at once to compromise the unity and then logically the equality of the divine being" (IV/1, 195, rev.). This question will continue to dog Barth's discussion. Does Barth in fact compromise the Son's unity and equality with the Father?

In a daring move Barth posits "an obedience that takes place in God" (IV/1, 195). It must be understood, he insists, as an obedience that does not compromise the Father and the Son either in their essential oneness or in their absolute coequality (IV/1, 196–97). To revert to some traditional terminology, it is not a matter of their *ousia* (being) but rather of a *taxis* (order) within it. It is a *taxis* that points to "the mystery of the deity of Christ" (IV/1, 197). Within their eternal

Godhead, Barth states, the Father and the Son are completely one and equal while yet also functionally distinct.

Modalism and subordinationism are the threats to be avoided at this point. Three affirmations about the full deity of Christ are therefore advanced that Barth says must be upheld "at all costs" (IV/1, 197).

1. Jesus Christ must be seen as the acting Subject who reconciles the world to God. If he were less than fully God, he would not be "a legitimate Subject competent to act in this matter. . . . When we have to do with Jesus Christ we have to do with God. What he does is a work which can only be God's own work, and not the work of another" (IV/1, 198).

Any "subordinationism" of the Son to the Father is therefore ruled out because the Son's work of reconciliation cannot possibly be the work of a lesser God. Not the slightest suggestion is made here that the Son needs to "constitute" himself as God by completing this work. He can only complete it if he is already fully God.

2. In the work of reconciliation, God must enter into the world and therefore into "the reality which is distinct from himself." He must enter into it as "the true God." The "being of the one true God" is present and active in Jesus Christ. Through his "most proper and direct" presence in Jesus Christ, God exercises his sovereign power by abolishing sin and death "in his own person." "Modalism" is thereby ruled out because God does not remain aloof in eternity, merely touching the world like a tangent to a circle (IV/1, 198).

In reconciliation, God in his "true and proper being" does not remain behind Jesus Christ in detachment. "We have to do with an economy in which God is truly himself and himself acts and intervenes in the world. Otherwise the atonement made in this economy is not a true atonement" (IV/1, 198). God enters into the world as the true God, in his true and proper being. He does so not in order to constitute himself but rather to move the world from within. By so moving the world he converts it to himself.

3. For the sake of reconciliation, the true God makes himself to be "identical" with the man Jesus (IV/1, 199). God's presence and action are "identical with the existence of the humiliated, lowly, and obedient man Jesus of Nazareth." In the person of Jesus, God "humbles himself and becomes lowly and obedient." He does so without entering into

"contradiction to his divine nature" and without encroaching on his eternal majesty (IV/1, 199).[16]

God indeed remains "high, almighty, eternal, righteous, and glorious—not also but precisely in his lowliness" (IV/1, 191, rev.). He allows himself to become lowly and humiliated in time while doing so "in agreement with . . . his divine nature" (IV/1, 199). No matter how difficult it may be to comprehend, we must take "the humiliation and lowliness and supremely the obedience of Christ" into our conception of "the proper being of the one true God." God's antecedent nature in eternity must be understood on the basis of the Son's obedience in the economy (IV/1, 199).[17]

Subordinationism and modalism are in effect evasions of the cross (IV/1, 199). The former thinks that the crucified Christ is a being "distinct from God," while the latter supposes that he is merely a "mode of appearance of the one true God" (IV/1, 200). What neither can tolerate, Barth argues, is the recognition that lowliness, humility, and obedience are inherent to God's essential nature. They deny the antecedent, eternal condition that makes Christ's humiliation possible as it culminates in the cross.

At this point the names of Athanasius and Nicaea are invoked. They were correct, Barth states, in rejecting subordinationism and modalism (IV/1, 200). They were right not to take offense "where no offense must be taken." The path that they charted was "the right way at that time." Although today their way cannot simply be repeated without further thought, they remind us "in which direction we have to look." Barth acknowledges that he is pursuing a path "formally independent" of them. Materially, however, he intends "to go further in [their] direction." He means to go beyond Athanasius and Nicaea without going against them (IV/1, 200). He understands his relation to them as one of solidarity.

16. When Barth states that God becomes "identical" with the human Jesus, he does not mean this in a reductive or absolute way. He means that the two are one "without the transformation of the one into the other, the admixture of the one with the other, or separation or division between them" (IV/3, 40). The two are "identical" in the sense of being inseparably one, but they never lose their abiding distinction. It is always a matter of unity-in-distinction and identity-in-difference. Barth's use of the term *identical* in volume IV is consistently misread by the revisionists.

17. This is not the same as saying, however, that God's antecedent nature must be defined *in terms of* the Son's obedience in the economy.

Can obedience be posited within God's own proper being? Can it be affirmed as something "essential to the being of God" (IV/1, 200)? Can there be "in God himself an above and a below, a *prius* and a *posterius*, a superiority and a subordination" (IV/1, 200–201)? No matter how perplexing it may seem, Barth maintains that within God's essential being there is indeed an unexpected element: "a below, a *posterius*, a subordination." If we reason from below to above, from time to eternity, we can see "that it belongs to the inner life of God that there should take place within it obedience" (IV/1, 201).

Obedience is not just an earthly event undertaken in the economy. On the contrary, "we have to reckon with such an event even in the being and life of God himself" (IV/1, 201). The event of obedience does not just occur as "an event in some . . . creaturely sphere." Nor does it involve "a mere appearance" when it occurs in eternity. Divine obedience is no less real in eternity than it is in the economy. Moreover, it can occur in the economy only through its antecedence in eternity.

The thesis is therefore ventured that God's eternal "divine oneness [*Einheit*] consists in the fact that in himself [God] is both One who is obeyed and Another who obeys" (IV/1, 201, rev.). Just as Athanasius had defined the divine oneness (*ousia*) as the Father begetting the Son, so Barth now goes a step further. The divine oneness, he suggests, consists not only in the Father begetting the Son but also in the Son obeying the Father.

In explaining this difficult thesis Barth presupposes his standard ontological distinction between God and the world. As the Creator, God coexists with the creature, without in any sense needing the creature. In particular, God does not need the creature in order to constitute himself as God. Nor does God need the creature in order to have a partner for the sake of fellowship in love and freedom. As the eternal Trinity, God already enjoys fellowship within himself (*koinonia*). Moreover, as superabundant in glory, God is already self-sufficient in himself (*aseitas*). Barth writes,

> God did not need this otherness of the world and man. In order not to be alone, single, enclosed within himself, God did not need coexistence with the creature. He does not will and posit the creature necessarily, but in freedom, as the basic act of his grace.

> His whole relationship to what is outside himself—its basis and history from first to last—rests on this fact [of not needing the creature]. For everything that the creature seems to offer him—its otherness, its being in antithesis to himself and therefore his own existence in co-existence—he has also in himself [eternally] as God, as the original and essential determination of his being and life as [the triune] God.
>
> Without the creature he has *all this originally in himself*, and it is his *free grace*, and *not an urgent necessity* to stand in a relationship of reciprocity to something other outside himself, if he allows the creature to participate in it—if, as it were, *in superfluity* he allows [the creature's] existence as another, as a counterpart to himself, and his own co-existence with it.
>
> In superfluity—we have to say this because we are in fact dealing with *an overflowing, not with a filling up of the perfection of God which needs no filling*. (IV/1, 201, rev.; italics added)[18]

This statement stands in a clear divergence from the "strong" (revisionist) view. Here in IV/1 we have Barth saying in his own words that God does not need the world in order to be God, that God relates to the world not out of some inner necessity but purely in an act of free grace, that God is not filling up a perfection that needs no filling, but that God allows his antecedent perfection to overflow toward the world in a gracious superfluity. "We are in fact dealing with an overflowing, not with a filling up of the perfection of God which needs no filling" [*nicht um eine Ergänzung der Vollkommenheit Gottes geht, die einer solchen nicht bedürftig ist*] (IV/1, 201).[19] The triune God is perfectly complete and determinate in and of himself.

"*Primarily, originally and properly* [*Zuerst, original, eigentlich*; i.e., not secondarily, subsequently, and derivatively] . . . God is all this in himself" (IV/1, 201, original italics restored). Primarily, originally, and properly, God as the Holy Trinity "is both One and also Another, his own counterpart, co-existent with himself" (IV/1, 201). Primarily, originally, and properly, God is always already complete in himself, in glorious abundance to all eternity. The triune God has no need to

18. I have reformatted this long quotation for easier reading.

19. Barth typically associates *Vollkommenheit* (perfection) with *Selbständigkeit* (self-sufficiency). See for example, *KD* IV/1, 328; cf. *CD* IV/1, 298.

constitute himself or perfect himself in the economy. His divine fullness is something antecedent, not consequent.

Within this essential divine fullness, Barth asserts, we can posit that the triune God exists "as a first and a second, above and below, *a priori* and *a posteriori*" (IV/1, 201–2). God's eternal and antecedent oneness is not a oneness of mere sameness. It is rather a oneness "which is open and free and active in itself—a oneness in more than one mode of being, a unity of the One with Another, of a first with a second, an above with a below, an origin and its consequences. It is a dynamic and living oneness, not a dead and static" monotony (IV/1, 202, rev.). The triune God lives in a dynamic oneness of differentiated unity to all eternity.

For Barth, God's eternal *ousia* (being) includes, as we have noted, a certain *taxis* (order) within itself. The *homoousia* between the Father and the Son does not exclude but includes an element of functional (but not ontological) subordination. Within "the one equal Godhead," the Son's functional subordination "has its own dignity." It does not "involve an inferiority, and therefore a deprivation, a lack." On the contrary, it involves "a particular being in glory." It involves no gradation, degradation, or inferiority in God (IV/1, 202). This *taxis* describes a freely affirmed super- and subordination between the Father and the Son coexisting as unabridged equals in love to all eternity.[20]

Starting from below with the obedience of Jesus Christ in the economy, Barth reasons that we cannot avoid "the astonishing conclusion" of a divine obedience in eternity. He reiterates that this is an "astounding deduction." By virtue of the doctrine of antecedence, however, he argues that this very deduction is what provides the eternal basis for the Son's temporal obedience. The Son's obedience in

20. Unfortunately Barth does not hesitate to illustrate this inner-trinitarian subordination by appealing to the subordination of "the wife to her husband" (IV/1, 202), as if the divine subordination that he posits were not something unique and incommunicable. As Kevin Giles points out, his remarks in this passage have been used to argue for the permanent subordination of the wife to the husband. See Giles, *Jesus and the Father* (Grand Rapids: Zondervan, 2006), chap. 8. For views more nuanced than Barth's, see Katherine Sonderegger, "Barth and Feminism," in *The Cambridge Companion to Karl Barth*, ed. John Webster (Cambridge: Cambridge University Press, 2000), 258–73; Clifford Green, "Liberation Theology? Karl Barth on Women and Men," *Union Seminary Quarterly Review* 29 (1974): 221–31.

eternity is the condition for the possibility of his obedience in the economy. The eternal Father is the one who "rules and commands in majesty" while the eternal Son is the one who "obeys in humility" (IV/1, 202). What takes place in obedience in the economy reiterates the inner life of the Trinity.

Barth now turns to the role of the Holy Spirit in God's inner life. It is the Spirit's role to uphold the essential oneness and equality that exist between the Father and the Son. Exactly as stated in previous volumes, it is the Holy Spirit who "makes possible and maintains" God's eternal fellowship (*koinonia*) with himself "without division or contradiction" (IV/1, 203; cf. I/1, 480; II/2, 101). The Spirit dwells in each divine "person," maintaining the oneness of each with the other as they coexist not only in mutual communion (*perichoresis*) but also in functional priority and subordination (*taxis*).

In this section, Barth proceeds to speak of the eternal relationship of the Father to the Son, and of the Son to the Father, as a "history." The context makes it clear that he is thinking of an intra-divine event. He is thinking of an eternal history, not (as might be mistaken) of an earthly history.[21]

Barth uses the word *history* here at a point where the tradition might ordinarily refer to God's being (*ousia*). For Barth, a certain "history" structures God's eternal being. The indivisible divine *ousia* is intrinsically complex. It is not only relational but in some sense also dynamic and historical. Barth writes, "The true and living God is the One whose Godhead [*ousia*] consists in this history, who is in these three modes of being the One God, the Eternal, the Almighty, the Holy, the Merciful, the One who loves in his freedom and is free in his love" (IV/1, 203).

In his antecedent trinitarian being God is concrete and alive. His being is not static but dynamic. It is self-moved to all eternity. It does not first become living and concrete when it enters into the economy. It already possesses these aspects and is therefore uniquely "historical" in itself. Relative to creaturely historicity, God's eternal historicity is "qualitatively different" (*qualitativ Andere*). It is "superior and majestic" (*Überlegene, Majestätische*). For the later Barth as for the earlier Barth, God's being is "Wholly Other" (*qualitativ Andere*) in eternity (IV/1, 176).

21. The "strong" (revisionist) reading runs aground at this point.

The "Wholly Other" God stands in an "indissoluble antithesis to . . . the whole cosmos" (*qualitativ Andere . . . in unaufhebbarer Gegenüberstellung . . . zum ganzen Kosmos*) (IV/1, 161).[22] The otherness of God in eternity is the presupposition of everything that God does in the economy. "If in Christ—even in the humiliated Christ born in a manger at Bethlehem and crucified on the cross of Golgotha—God is not unchanged and wholly God, then everything that we may say about the reconciliation of the world made by God in this humiliated One is left hanging in the air" (IV/1, 183). If God ceased to be God—if he ceased to be undivided, holy, and immortal in himself—we could not be reconciled to him, precisely because he would have ceased to be God.

Therefore, even in his self-humiliation, even to the point of death on the cross, God remains unchanged in himself and is wholly God.

> God gives himself, but he does not give himself away. He does not give up being God in becoming a creature, in becoming man. He does not cease to be God. He does not come into conflict with himself. He does not sin when in unity with the man Jesus he mingles with sinners and takes their place. And when he dies in his unity with this man, death does not gain any power over him. He exists as God in the righteousness and the life, the obedience and the resurrection of this man. He makes his own the being of man in contradiction against him, but he does not capitulate to it [*er macht ihn aber nicht mit*]. He also makes his own the being of man under the curse of this contradiction, but in order to do away with it as he suffers it. He acts as Lord over this contradiction even as he subjects himself to it. (IV/1, 185, rev.)

God's being does not belong to created time, and yet it includes within itself its own unique mode of uncreated time. This inner divine time is described as the "true time." As such it functions as the prototype

22. In context these statements about God as *qualitativ Andere* are made about the deity of the incarnate Son, but they would apply ipso facto to God's deity as such. On the other hand, Barth rules out the idea that God's deity is merely an abstraction. It would be an abstraction if God were "*ganz Andere*" in the sense of being absolute as over against everything relative, exalted as over against everything lowly, and lofty as over against everything humble (IV/1, 186). On the contrary, the otherness of the Wholly Other God includes these apparent opposites within itself. It contains within itself the prototype of everything that God posits as relative, lowly, and humble outside himself.

of all created time. It is a condition for the possibility of the incarnation, even as the incarnation reveals it as the mystery of a distinctive divine temporality in eternity.

"The eternity in which [God] himself is true time and the Creator of all time," writes Barth, "is revealed in the fact that, although our time is that of sin and death, he can enter it and himself be temporal in it, yet without ceasing to be eternal, able rather to be the Eternal in time" (IV/1, 187–88). God enters into the world of sin without ceasing to be holy. He enters into the composite and the transitory creation without ceasing to be undivided and immutable. He enters into suffering and death without ceasing to be impassible and immortal. And just so, God enters into time without ceasing to be eternal.

The eternity of "the true and living God" is such that God's eternal Godhead (*ousia*) consists in a "history." It is a history that takes place in his "three [trinitarian] modes of being" [*hypostases*]. It takes place within the very Godhead of "the Eternal, the Almighty, the Holy, the Merciful, the One who loves in his freedom and is free in his love" (IV/1, 203). As Barth sees it, God's eternal "history" is the one true, original, and self-sufficient history. As such, it serves as the prototype of all earthly history.

All that God does *ad extra*—his speaking, activity, and work—consists in the fact "that he gives to the world created by him, to man, a part in the history in which he is God" (IV/1, 203). What God does *ad extra* is not what makes him historical. Rather, the trinitarian history in which he lives to all eternity—on his side, so to speak, of the ontological divide—is what he determines to share with the creature. He determines to share it as the final goal of his work of redemption. The fallen creature as redeemed in Christ is destined to receive a share in "the inner life of God himself" (IV/1, 203).

The creature's participation in God is "the goal and end of [God's] whole activity as established at its beginning" (IV/1, 203). It is the goal of redemption as established in election and made effectual by means of reconciliation. It is the goal accomplished through the earthly obedience of the Son. By the Son's death, the fallen creature is rescued from death and elevated to eternal life. In Christ, the fallen creature is judged and redeemed in order to be given "a part in the history in which [God] is God" (IV/1, 203).

In reconciling the world to himself, God allows "the inward divine relationship" between the Father and the Son to be "identical" in essence with "the very different relationship" that is established between the Son and Jesus (IV/1, 203). In "his mode of being as the one who is obedient in humility," God allows himself to become a human being in order to accomplish reconciliation. He goes into the "far country"—the realm of creatureliness, sin, and death. He adds to himself what did not previously belong to him.

For Barth, the event of the incarnation is new even for God. "He becomes what he had not previously been. He takes into unity with his divine being a quite different, a creaturely and indeed a sinful being. To do this he empties himself, he humbles himself. But, as in his action as Creator, he does not do it apart from its basis in his own being, in his own inner life" (IV/1, 203).

God does not do all this "without any correspondence [*Entsprechung*] to . . . the [eternal] history in which he is God," as if what he undertakes in the economy had no prior basis in eternity. On the contrary, what God undertakes in the economy has "its basis in his own being, in his own inner life." Therefore, what God does in the economy can be described as the "miraculously consistent ultimate continuation" [*wunderbar konsequenter letzter Fortsetzung*] of "the history in which he is God" (IV/1, 203).[23]

What God does in the economy stands in continuity with what he is in eternity—miraculously (*wunderbar*). There is, contrary to revisionism, no simple line of continuity here. It is a continuity only in the midst of ontological discontinuity—the discontinuity between eternity and time—but it is indeed real continuity for all that by virtue of the miracle of divine grace. In this miracle God is not inconsistent with himself but rather corresponds to himself. As always in Barth, the language of "correspondence" suggests the asymmetrical unity-in-distinction between God's eternal being or "history" *ad intra* and the external form it assumes in the economy.[24]

23. The English translation is quite garbled here: "the strangely logical final continuation."

24. Note that Barth could speak about "God in himself" as the "immanent Trinity" in terms of the "eternal history of God" as early as the initial volume of the *Church Dogmatics*. "We make a deliberate and sharp distinction between the [economic]

The point to see is that Barth's doctrine of antecedence is in play. "[God] does not need to deny, let alone abandon and leave behind or even diminish his Godhead to do this" (IV/1, 203). The question is not, as the "strong" (revisionist) view would have it, whether the obedience of the Son in the far country serves to complete God's otherwise incomplete being, as if without his temporal obedience God would fail to be "constituted" as God. On the contrary, the question as Barth frames it is whether God can humble himself in the economy without diminishing his perfection in eternity. He answers that God can do so without contradicting himself because his eternal Godhead—the history in which he lives in and for himself—already contains within itself the aspects of humility and obedience.

In the far country God causes "his inner being as God" to take "outward form" in earthly history (IV/1, 204). In the second mode of his triune being, he is already obedient in humility. On that basis he can also become obedient in the form of a human being. He wills to be "not only the one God, but *also* this one man, and precisely as the one God to be this one man" (IV/1, 204, rev.; italics restored).[25] Who and what God is in eternity is reiterated in the economy.

Barth is making three main points here: (1) that who and what God is in eternity takes on a new, external form in time; (2) that this temporal form is freely chosen, being in no sense necessary for God to be God; and (3) that God can indeed take on this new form without compromising the perfection of his eternal Godhead because his Godhead already contains the elements of humility and obedience within itself.

God does not owe this external obedience and self-humiliation to the creature.

> He does not owe it even to himself. He owes it just as little and even less than he did to the creation. Neither in the one case [creation] nor in the other [reconciliation]—and even less in this case [reconciliation]—can there be any question of the necessary working of an inward divine

---

Trinity . . . and God's immanent Trinity, i.e., between 'God in Himself' and 'God for us,' between the 'eternal history of God' and his temporal acts" (I/1, 172).

25. Note that in the German original of this particular section, the word "also" [*auch*] is repeated more than ten times. It indicates that God is adding a new determination to his perfect being, not constituting it.

> mechanism, or a mechanism which controls the relationship of God and the world. (IV/1, 204)

In giving himself to the world in Christ, God is not driven by any inward necessity but remains who and what he is as God.

> He does not change in giving himself [*verändert sich nicht*]. He simply activates and reveals himself *ad extra* in the world [*betätigt und offenbart sich*]. He is in and for the world what he is in and for himself [*in und für sich selber*]. He is *also* in time what he is in eternity (and what he can be *also* in time because of his eternal being). (IV/1, 204, rev.; italics added)

The antecedent ground in eternity of the Son's obedience in the economy could not be made clearer. In surrendering himself to suffering and death for the sake of the world, the Son of God does not change (*verändert sich nicht*). He does not cease to be God. Nor does he constitute himself as God. He simply "activates and reveals himself" for who he is in a new and temporal form (*betätigt und offenbart sich*). The actually existing textual Barth once again stands opposed to the "strong" (revisionist) reading.

The temporal form of the Son's obedience corresponds to the eternal form that makes it possible. The two forms coexist (1) without separation or division, (2) without confusion or change, and (3) with the eternal form taking precedence over the temporal form (asymmetry). The eternal form would be entirely what it is without the temporal form, but the temporal form would be nothing without the eternal form. Given this irreversible asymmetry, the two forms coexist by grace in a pattern of unity-in-distinction. Moreover, the precedence, perfection, and self-sufficiency of the eternal form is what makes its relation to the temporal form irreversible. The temporal form is conditioned by the eternal form, but the eternal form is not conditioned by the temporal form.

The line of continuity between the two forms—the "miraculously consistent ultimate continuation" (IV/1, 203)—is based on "the true deity of Jesus Christ" (IV/1, 204). In this continuity he becomes as a human being what he already is as God. He becomes in the economy what he already is in eternity. Whether in time or in eternity, he is the one who is "obedient in humility" (IV/1, 204).

> He is in our lowliness what he is in his majesty (and what he can be also in our lowliness because his majesty is also lowliness). He is as man, as the man who is obedient in humility, Jesus of Nazareth, what he is as God (and what he can be also as man because he is it as God in this mode of divine being). That is the true deity of Jesus Christ, obedient in humility, in its unity and equality, its *homoousia*, with the deity of the One who sent him and to whom he is obedient. (IV/1, 204)

These words bring us to the "first ending" in IV/1, 192–210. Materially, Barth has set forth his main points, especially that God's eternal being (*ousia*) is constituted by a kind of dynamic "history" in which the Son is eternally obedient to the Father without compromising the ontological equality of their common deity. The second ending, or perhaps the coda, which Barth proceeds to unfold, is largely a kind of reprise. He now restates in more traditional terms what he has already stated in his actualistic idiom. Actualism in Barth is a motif, not an ideology or an ontological system. He can use it to make his points, and he prefers to do so, but he is not necessarily bound to it. He can say what he wants to say without it. That is what he does in the second ending.

As a bridge between the two endings, Barth writes,

> For the basis, development and explanation of the doctrine of the Trinity in its own context and in all its details, and for an understanding of its exegetical and historical implications, we must refer back to *CD* I/1 § 8–12. We have here approached this first and final Christian truth [the Trinity] from a special standpoint, and in this context we can speak of it only briefly, selectively, and in a limited way. (IV/1, 204)

What Barth has presented so far in IV/1 regarding the inner life of the Trinity has been developed from "a special standpoint." He has examined the Trinity in both the economy and in eternity with an eye toward the obedience of the Son. He has argued that the Son's temporal obedience is grounded in his prior eternal obedience. "He is . . . for the world what he is in and for himself. He is also in time what he is in eternity (and what he can be also in time because of his eternal being)" (IV/1, 204, rev.). Barth has applied his doctrine of antecedence.

He has also suggested that this "special standpoint" stands in continuity with Athanasius and Nicaea. Like them, he has rejected subordinationism and modalism. Also like them, he has affirmed the oneness and coequality of the Father and the Son with respect to their eternal being (*ousia*) while still allowing (in a way that goes beyond them) that the Father and the Son are differentiated, in part, by a certain ordering (*taxis*). (Barth has so far presupposed, but not discussed, that the two are also differentiated by virtue of their relations of origin, as he developed that point in I/1.) He has presupposed his essential agreement with Athanasius and Nicaea while addressing questions they did not discuss (IV/1, 200).

Barth now explicitly reaffirms what the "strong" (revisionist) reading thinks he has long since set aside. He reaffirms the doctrine of the Trinity as he developed it in I/1. He asserts that in IV/1 he has only developed his previous insights from a special standpoint. He has not broken with his original doctrine of the Trinity. He has not suggested but openly denied that God's being is under some kind of temporal construction. He has aligned himself with the main aspects of the historic ecumenical tradition. For the "strong" (revisionist) reading, all this is, to say the least, inconvenient.

Since the "thoroughly modern, post-metaphysical Barth" could not have embraced Athanasius and Nicaea (as he does in this passage from IV/1) without encumbering himself with elements of "classical theism," it will be worthwhile to revisit some points that Barth made in I/1. Of particular interest is the section where Barth follows Athanasius (and John of Damascus) by describing God's begetting of the Son as a "work of nature" as over against God's distinctive "work of will" in creating the world (ἔργον φύσεως / ἔργον θελήσεως). Barth accepts this distinction but with qualifications. In line with Aquinas (and Hilary), he affirms that the divine begetting is a "work of nature" while also being in some sense a "work of will."

> The begetting of the Son is certainly to be understood as an act of divine will, but only as the act of will in which *Deus vult se esse Deum* [God wills himself to be God], as the act of will in which God, in freedom of course, wills himself and, in virtue of this will of his, is himself. In this sense, identically indeed with God's being himself, the begetting of the Son is also an ἔργον θελήσεως [work of will] for here θέλησις [will] and φύσις [nature] are one and the same. (I/1, 435)

The subtle interplay between will and nature in this remark is worthy of note. It is precisely this kind of subtlety that the "strong" (revisionist) reading seems to ride over roughshod. Revisionism would insist that for Barth God's nature is merely a function of his will, that the form taken by his nature is discretionary, that God might or might not have been trinitarian, and that his trinitarian nature is the result of a pretemporal decision, namely, that of election. There is no trace of these ideas, of course, in Athanasius and Nicaea. Nor is there any trace of them in I/1. With no hint of hesitation, Barth now refers back in IV/1 to what he had affirmed in I/1 in accord with Athanasius and Nicaea.

In I/1 Barth develops the distinction Athanasius made between a "work of nature" and a "work of will" in a way that runs counter to revisionism.

> But the begetting of the Son is not an act of the divine will in the way that freedom to will this or that is expressed in the concept of will. God has this latter freedom in respect of creation—he is free to will it or not to will it—and creation is thus an ἔργον θελήσεως [work of will].
>
> But he does not have this freedom in respect of his being God. God cannot not be God. Therefore—and this is the same thing—he cannot not be Father and cannot be without the Son. His freedom or aseity in respect of himself consists in his freedom, not determined by anything but himself, to be God, and that means to be the Father of the Son.
>
> A freedom to be able not to be this would be an abrogation of his freedom. Thus the begetting of the Son is an ἔργον φύσεως [work of nature]. It could not not happen just as God could not not be God, whereas creation is an ἔργον θελήσεως [work of will] in the sense that it could also not happen and yet God would not on that account be any the less God. (I/1, 435, rev.)[26]

Barth accepts the Athanasian distinction between a "work of nature" and a "work of will," modifying it only to the extent of incorporating the idea of will into the work of nature. But the spirit of the distinction is upheld.[27] Creation is an act of will in a very different sense

26. I have revised the formatting here for easier reading.

27. Barth's subtle modification of this Athanasian distinction gives the lie to the idea that he regarded the triune God's being merely as "decision." See Robert W. Jenson,

than is the eternal begetting of the Son. The creation is something God is free to will or not to will. God could have decided not to will it without being any the less God (a point that Barth will constantly reiterate in his *Church Dogmatics* from beginning to end). But God cannot will not to be God. And that means God cannot will not to be the Father, because God just is (as Athanasius taught) the Father begetting the Son. Whatever it means for God to be free, God is not free to annul himself as God. "He cannot not be Father and cannot be without the Son" (I/1, 435). God would abrogate his freedom if he failed to affirm himself freely. Who and what God is by nature—the Father begetting the Son in the unity of the Holy Spirit to all eternity—is just what God freely affirms himself to be. "For here θέλησις [will] and φύσις [nature] are one and the same" (I/1, 435).

God's nature is not a result of his will any more than his being is a result of his act. For Barth these paired terms (will/nature and being/act) always coexist in a pattern of coordination, not in a pattern of priority and subordination or of antecedence and consequence. Each of the paired terms is logically and ontologically basic. No matter which one we start with, the other is always already implicated in it irreducibly and primordially.

The same is true of the relationship between the Father and the Son. Logically speaking, "a" is prior to "b" if "a" can be defined without reference to "b." But the Son cannot be defined without reference to the Father, nor can the Father be defined without reference to the Son. Ontologically speaking, moreover, although the Son is "generated," and the Father is "ungenerated," they are one and coequal to all eternity. Therefore, neither one is logically or ontologically prior to the other. Relative to one another, they are each logically and ontologically basic.[28]

There is no evidence that Barth ever departed from this position. Indeed, there is good reason to believe, as we have seen, that he realigned himself with it in IV/1. In this very text, to which the "strong"

"Karl Barth on the Being of God," in *Thomas Aquinas and Karl Barth*, ed. Bruce L. McCormack and Thomas Joseph White (Grand Rapids: Eerdmans, 2013), 48–49.

28. Barth would not affirm "the monarchy of the Father" in any sense that rendered the Son and the Spirit logically and ontologically subordinate. For a good discussion, see David Guretzki, *Karl Barth on the Filioque* (Burlington, VT: Ashgate, 2009), 126–29.

(revisionist) view would appeal for confirmation, Barth associates himself with Athanasius, Nicaea, and his own original doctrine of the Trinity as set forth in I/1, sections 8–12. None of this is taken into account by the "strong" reading, which posits that Barth essentially broke with these ideas in II/2.

Let us return to Barth's "second ending." Having "refrained from using the concepts which dominate the New Testament and ecclesiastical dogma," Barth writes, "we can now introduce them" (IV/1, 204). He opens with a summary statement: "Jesus Christ is the Son of God who became man, who as such is One with God the Father, equal to him in deity, by the Holy Spirit, in whom the Father affirms and loves him and he the Father, in a mutual fellowship" (IV/1, 204).

Here, in traditional language, three points are implicit: (1) the one indivisible divine *ousia*, (2) the three divine *hypostases*, and (3) their mutual *perichoresis*. This is who and what God is to all eternity, first antecedently in himself and then (on that basis) also in relation to the world. God's activation and revelation of himself in the world presuppose his perfect and self-sufficient being (*aseitas*) in eternity.

Barth begins by reflecting on the term "person" as a translation for the term *hypostasis*. He reiterates a point made in his first volume (I/1, 355–60). The "persons" of the Trinity cannot be understood as three centers of consciousness.

> It was never intended to imply—at any rate in the main stream of theological tradition—that there are in God three different personalities, three self-existent individuals with their own special self-consciousness, cognition, volition, activity, effects, revelation, and name. The one name of the one God is the threefold name of Father, Son, and Holy Spirit. The one "personality" of God, the one active and speaking divine Ego, is Father, Son, and Holy Spirit. Otherwise we should obviously have to speak of three gods. And this is what the Early Church not only would not do, but in the conception of the doctrine of the Trinity which ultimately prevailed, [the Early Church] tried expressly to exclude, just as it did any idea of a division or inequality between Father, Son and Holy Spirit. Christian faith and the Christian confession has one Subject, not three. (IV/1, 205)

The one God exists in and only in his three modes of being. He exists to all eternity in his self-repetition as the Father, the Son, and the Holy Spirit. These are the three distinct modes of the one indivisible God. He exists in them (not behind or above them) as a single acting Subject. "He does not exist as such outside or behind or above these modes of being. He does not exist otherwise than as Father, Son, and Holy Spirit. He exists in their mutual interconnection and relationship" (IV/1, 205).

God exists in these three distinct modes to all eternity as the living God. His existence in and for himself is dynamic, not static. On the basis of his triune identity—of his eternal, living, and relational being—God is also the Lord of the world. He works in relation to the world as Creator, Reconciler, and Redeemer. He is first the Father, the Son, and the Holy Spirit in himself and then again also with respect to the world.

The core affirmations in IV/1 bear repeating. "[God] is also in time what he is in eternity," and it is "because of his eternal being" that he can be what he is in time (IV/1, 204). "*Er ist nur auch in der Zeit, was er in Ewigkeit ist (und gerade vermöge seines ewigen Seins auch in der Zeit sein kann)*" (*KD* IV/1, 223). "His being as God"—in eternity and then also in time—"is his being in his own history" (IV/1, 205). "*Sein Sein als Gott ist Sein im Geschehen dieser seiner eigenen Geschichte*" (*KD* IV/1, 224). God's being is a living history "in and for himself" (*in und für sich selber*), which is then reiterated through his intervention in the world (IV/1, 204; *KD* IV/1, 223; cf. IV/1, 210). The fundamental distinctions (the ontological divide) between the immanent Trinity and the economic Trinity, between the Creator and the creature, between eternity and time—indeed between antecedence and subsequence—are upheld throughout. The ontological divide, though ineffaceable, is no obstacle to the workings of grace. As in I/1, so also in IV/1: what God is in himself to all eternity serves as the basis for his work in the economy.

Barth proceeds to reflect on the ontological otherness of God. God's otherness, he observes, creates real difficulties for theological language. All our terms for God, even at their best, are "but inadequate expressions" (IV/1, 205). Because none of them can "comprehend or exhaust" God's reality, the church has always confessed "the incomprehensibility of God." As Augustine says, "If God, it is not comprehensible"; if comprehensible, it is not God.[29] It is always a matter of comprehending the incomprehensibility of God in his incomprehensibility. This is certainly the case when it comes to "the triune being of God and especially of his three modes of being." The church has always been aware that with terms like Father, Son, and Holy Spirit, "it can only aim at the real thing which is in question" (IV/1, 205).

Comprehending Jesus Christ as "the Son of God"—especially regarding his obedience, whether in its eternal aspect or its temporal aspect—is no exception. To say that Jesus Christ is "God's Son" means that he is unlike any Son that we know. We have to use an ordinary word to describe an ineffable reality that is unique in kind. Following the New Testament, we have to use the word "Son" in such a way as "to bring out the singularity and the uniqueness of this Subject and therefore of his work" (IV/1, 206).

What can be meant when we speak of Jesus Christ as the Son of God? Barth will approach this question from more than one angle. His first answer again departs from revisionism. There is no sense in which Jesus Christ can be spoken of as God's Son, Barth argues, as if he were "begotten in time" (IV/1, 206). He cannot have been begotten in time because he was already begotten in eternity. "*There is no question of a temporal event in which he* began *to be the Son of God*" (IV/1, 206, italics added).[30] It follows that there can be no question of a temporal event by which he "constitutes" himself as the Son. He does not need to be constituted in time (or with reference to time) because he is already constituted to all eternity.

Barth illustrates this point by referring to the doctrine of the virgin birth. This doctrine is essentially about Jesus Christ as the Son of God. "It is not a statement about how he became this, a statement concerning the basis and condition of his divine Sonship. It is a description of the way in which the Son of God became man. . . . This

29. "*Si comprehendis, non est Deus.*" Augustine, *Sermo* 117.3.5. Quoted by Barth, II/1, 185.

30. "*Es ist, wenn es um Jesus Christus geht, nichts mit einem solchen zeitlichen Ereignis, in welchem er erst angefangenhätte, Gottes Sohn zu sein*" (*KD* IV/1, 226). This is essentially the same point that we have seen Barth make elsewhere (I/1, 427; II/2, 107; IV/2, 53–54).

event is not the basis of the fact that the One who there became man was the Son of God" (IV/1, 207).

Relative to his temporal advent, the status of Jesus's divine Sonship must be understood as antecedent rather than as subsequent. The divine Son was already constituted as such before becoming human in time. The virgin birth is said to make this point. Mary was sanctified by God, writes Barth, to become the mother of his Son. "It is [God] who makes his Son hers, and in that way shares with humanity in her person nothing less than his own existence" (IV/1, 207). It is an act of God's sharing his existence (already of course metaphysically complete), not of constituting it.

What the virgin birth attests (much like the empty tomb after Jesus's rising from the dead) is "the mystery of the incarnation" (IV/1, 207). Barth adds, "These attestations"—the virgin birth and the empty tomb—"are based on his divine Sonship, not his divine Sonship on these attestations" (IV/1, 207). "They have a great deal to do with it [his divine Sonship] noetically, but nothing at all ontically" (*noetisch sehr viel . . . aber ontisch nichts*) (IV/1, 207). In other words, they serve to reveal the Son for who he is while in no way constituting his reality. What Barth states here about the virgin birth and the empty tomb would apply *mutatis mutandis* to pretemporal election. The Son's reality is in no way "constituted" by it.

Barth's second approach to the mystery of Jesus's divine Sonship serves to radicalize an already radical position. To be God's Son means that Jesus Christ "is quite different from all other men" (IV/1, 208). Given his true humanity, what is it that distinguishes him from all others? Barth answers, "It is his whole being to be this obedient One. This is what distinguishes him from all creatures either in heaven or earth" (IV/1, 208). To the extent that his obedience is "a divine and not a human work," it differentiates him as God's Son from all others (IV/1, 209). Obedience is not just something the Son does. It is something that he is. His whole raison d'être is to be obedient, first in eternity and then (on that basis) also in time. "It is his whole being to be this obedient One" (IV/1, 208).

Obedience is not just something that the Son undertakes in time. It is what defines "his whole being," in eternity (IV/1, 208). When he appears in human flesh, it is precisely his obedience that reveals him to be God's Son. Barth's point is again that the Son's earthly obedience is revelatory in status, not constitutive. "The fact that he shows himself to be the Son of God in this way does not mean that he becomes the Son of God thereby" (IV/1, 208). He cannot become the eternal Son in the economy (or with respect to his advent in time) because he is already the eternal Son in and of himself.

The Son's obedience is entirely parallel in status to his lordship. In his obedience he does something that "only God can do," and in his obedience he is something that only God can be (IV/1, 208–9). His obedience (like his lordship) is grounded and constituted by his eternal role within the Trinity.

The Father is "the self-positing God (the Father who eternally begets)" even as the Son is the "self-posited God (the eternally begotten of the Father as the dogma has it)" (IV/1, 209). Even in his humility the Son shares fully in the majesty of the Father. The Father is the eternal "origin," while the Son, as begotten, is the eternal "consequence." The Father who commands is never without the Son who obeys. "The One who eternally begets is never apart from the One who is eternally begotten. Nor is the latter apart from the former" (IV/1, 209). At the same time, neither of them is who he is "without a mutual affirmation and love in the Holy Spirit." The Holy Spirit enjoys this eternal role antecedently to and independently of his operation on earth. It would be incorrect to claim that for Barth the Spirit's constitutive raison d'être is the church.

In his earthly obedience the Son actually "shows himself to be the One he is" (IV/1, 209). He "shows, affirms, activates, and reveals himself" (IV/1, 209). He does not become something other than he was antecedently. Nor does he complete a divine identity as if it were in need of completion. He simply reveals himself in his obedience for who he is: "The Son of God, the one God in his mode of being as the Son" (IV/1, 209).

Trinitarian language about the "Son" must be understood in light of his radical otherness and ontological uniqueness. The term "Son" must be seen as indispensable and yet also at the same time as inadequate. It is indispensable because it is given normative status by revelation and because it is good enough to do the job it needs to do. It seems to have advantages that no alternative term quite manifests.

Barth outlines the serviceability of the term. It can convey the way in which a son is naturally subject to the authority of a father. It can convey that a father has the authority to expect certain behavior from his son, and that a son is obligated to respect his father's will. It can convey that a close relationship between them produces a certain unity in what they will and what they choose to achieve. Finally, it conveys that the father could not be a father without his offspring (in this case a son) and that the son could not be a son without his father. All this shows, according to Barth, "what the term can convey" (IV/1, 209).

What the term cannot convey, however, is the radical otherness of this sonship. Because it is unique in kind, it is unlike any sonship that we know. It differs from every other sonship in its ontological necessity, perfection, and eternity. The term cannot bring out the "ontological necessity" in which this particular Father and this particular Son enjoy a "perfection in which . . . they are one" (IV/1, 209). It cannot bring out that they are "different modes of being of one and the same personal God." It cannot convey "the eternity of the fatherly begetting and of the being begotten of the Son." (Barth here affirms the eternal perfection of this unique begetting and being begotten.) Nor can it bring out how the divine eternity "is the basis of their relationship." Eternity is what grounds "their free but also necessary fellowship and love in the activity of the Holy Spirit as the third divine mode of being of the same kind" (IV/1, 209). All this is said about the eternal Trinity in and of itself without any reference to election.

This eternal begetting and being begotten is also the basis of "the self-evident fulfillment of that *determination* [*Bestimmung*] of a son to his father, the actual rendering of a perfect obedience, the ceaseless unity of the One who disposes and the One who complies, the actual oneness and agreement of that which they will and do" (IV/1, 209–10, italics added). Barth's use of the term "determination" here is entirely intra-trinitarian, again with no reference to election. The Son is constituted by being eternally begotten of the Father and "determined" for obedience to him within the eternal Godhead. This obedience, perfectly rendered, is what expresses the "ceaseless unity" of the Father and the Son and their perfect agreement in all that they will and do. It is an obedience, agreement, and oneness antecedent to all God's ways and works with the world. This antecedent obedience, agreement, and oneness is what Barth had previously described in IV/1 as God's "history" in and for himself.

In concluding his remarks on the limitations of theological language, Barth points once again to this eternal divine history. It is a history unlike any other history, a history transcendent and ontologically unique. "The history in which God is the living God in himself can only be indicated but not conceived by our terms son and father and spirit" (IV/1, 210). Likewise, the term "Son" can only point to eternal mysteries that are essentially beyond our grasp. The term "Son" goes beyond anything that might be meant in its other applications. Nevertheless, "it deserves our every confidence because it is true." Whatever its inadequacies might be, it tells us that Jesus Christ is the eternal Son made flesh. Like all our language about the ineffable God as given normatively by revelation, it points away from itself "to the One who will himself tell those who have ears to hear who he is" (IV/1, 210).

Conclusion

No doubt can exist that what Barth says in IV/1, 192–210, is entirely consistent with what he says in the passage cited at the outset from IV/2, 345 (and with many other passages, early and late). In both cases—and this is the key point at issue—the fullness (*aseitas*) of the eternal Trinity's inner life is the basis for all God's ways and works in the world. God reiterates in time "what he is in eternity," and it is "because of his eternal being" that he can also take temporal form (IV/1, 204). As in any standard Nicene theology, the Son is constituted by his being begotten eternally of the Father (IV/1, 209–10). "There is no question of a temporal event in which he began to be the Son of God" (IV/1, 206). Barth's views on this matter remained unchanged from the beginning of the *Church Dogmatics* to the end.

The "strong" (revisionist) charge of "inconsistency," as leveled in particular by Professor Nimmo, has proven to be ill considered. The "weak" (traditionalist) reading, on the other hand, can not only satisfy the principle of charity but also rest its case on a detailed engagement with the actually existing textual Barth. The "strong" view, which can do neither of these things, has turned out to be weak while the "weak" view has turned out to be strong.

4

Two Disputed Points

The Obedience of the Son and Classical Theism

Barth's View Critically Assessed

Perhaps this is the place to reiterate that the driving interest of this book has to do with Karl Barth, not with revisionism. It is my hope that the book might be of some value for students of Barth even after revisionism vanishes from the scene (as it will). Revisionism is of little interest in its own right. It claims attention mainly as an example of how not to read Karl Barth. If only the revisionists would cease ascribing their views to Barth, they would have nothing to fear from his more careful readers.

Barth's proposal about the obedience of the Son, however, is not beyond question. Even within his own premises, one may wonder about the wisdom of arguing that obedience is constitutive of the Son's essential deity. Obedience belongs to the Son's eternal essence, Barth has argued, regardless of its being activated in time.

The position Barth takes is motivated by his doctrine of antecedence. According to that doctrine, God does nothing in time that does not reflect his antecedent being in eternity. "What he is in revelation he is antecedently in himself" (I/1, 466). God reiterates in time what he is in himself, and what he is in himself forms the basis of his temporal activity. In other words, God enters into time, even into sin and death, without ceasing to be God. And he can do so freely because he is sovereign and under no compulsion to do so. Because of who and what he is in self-sufficiency, he can be the same also for us. He is free to enter the world for the sake of his love, and his love always comes as a gift.

On this basis Barth reasons from below to above. He reasons from the Son of God's obedience in the far country back into the Trinity's inner life. He draws inferences from time to eternity. If the Son is obedient in time, he must already have been so in eternity, and his eternal obedience must be constitutive of his deity. His eternal obedience, it is thought, provides the condition for the possibility of his temporal obedience. He could not be obedient in the economy were he not already obedient in eternity. That is how Barth reasons. But does his conclusion really make sense?

It is one of Barth's great insights that God is the One who loves in freedom. God's being in act, his being as the One who loves, and his being in freedom—all these elements constitute his inner life as the triune God. On this basis God can also be in the economy what he is eternally in himself: the One who loves in freedom.

One wonders, however, why God's being in love and freedom as such should not be sufficient to ground all that he does in time. Assuming the validity of Barth's doctrine of antecedence, why should the correspondence between time and eternity need to be such a tight fit? Why isn't the love and freedom of the eternal Trinity a sufficient ground in itself for the Son's emptying of himself, for his taking the form of a slave, for his becoming obedient to the point of death, even death on a cross?

In particular, why shouldn't the Son's eternal love for the Father in the Spirit (and their common love for the world) take on this extraordinary form in extremis? Why shouldn't the line of continuity from eternity to time simply be love—that "miraculously consistent ultimate continuation" (IV/1, 203)—as opposed to strictly "obedience"? Why shouldn't we think of the eternal Son's love for the Father as sufficient to constitute his identity (as eternally begotten)?

Why shouldn't his radical obedience in time be seen merely as love's contingent and contextualized expression? Why should the Son's functional subordination to the Father in time require a similar subordination to all eternity? In short, why shouldn't love itself and love alone (in freedom) be enough to satisfy Barth's doctrine of antecedence?[1]

This is not a new question about how Barth works out his doctrine. It might be asked about the earlier Barth as well as the later one. For example, consider the way Barth reads grace back into the eternal being of God. He has argued in II/1 that divine grace means the condescension of a superior to an inferior. Grace also means taking every measure to overcome whatever opposition, resistance, and hostility that may exist in the one chosen to be its recipient. It means attacking and wiping out sin at its root (II/1, 354–56).

If all this is true about the definition of grace, how can Barth say that before God acts graciously *ad extra*, his antecedent being must include grace in itself? How can he say that "grace is the very essence of the being of God" (II/1, 356)? Barth, who raises this question himself, answers,

> One might object that in his own being there cannot be a creature standing over against him, still less any opposition from this other, and therefore that there cannot take place any special turning, or condescension, or overcoming of the resistance of the other, and consequently that there cannot be any scope for grace.
>
> Our reply is that there is not in fact any scope for *the* form which grace takes in its manifestations to us. The form in which grace exists in God himself . . . is in point of fact hidden from us and incomprehensible to us. . . .
>
> How then can it be denied that primarily [grace] is real in God himself in a form which is concealed from us and incomprehensible to us—in him who as Father, Son and Holy Spirit is One, who is utterly at one in himself, in whom therefore there is neither the need nor the

1. Barth might arguably have done better to stay with his earlier view: "For all the rich differentiation of God, there is no higher and lower in his unity, no prior and posterior in his individual perfections. There is order in God, but no subordination or superordination" (III/2, 371). I cannot see that Barth's doctrine of antecedence would have required anything more.

> capacity for any turning and condescension, in whom there is no strife and therefore no reconciliation? (II/1, 357–58, original italics restored)[2]

Regardless of what one makes of this argument, it could be applied to what Barth says in IV/1 about the Son's obedience to all eternity. The application would run as follows. There is no scope in eternity for the specific form assumed by the Son's obedience in the economy. There is no place in eternity for abject shame, agony, and death. The Son's antecedent obedience must occur, if at all, in a very different form—a form that is "hidden from us and incomprehensible to us" (II/1, 357). The eternal obedience of the Son must differ from any obedience that we know.

Nevertheless, one could still argue, as I have suggested, that both grace and obedience are better seen as extraordinary determinations of God's primordial love and freedom. Why shouldn't the freedom of God's love within the eternal Godhead be more than sufficient to ground the special forms taken in extremis to rescue a perishing world? If we let love and freedom as such be the eternal basis of God's external works, then the intention behind Barth's antecedence doctrine would still be upheld. God would still be the same God of love and freedom for us that he is antecedently in himself. The perplexing claim that grace and obedience, as Barth has defined them, belong essentially to God's inner life would be avoided. However, since he posits that they occur in eternity in forms beyond all understanding, perhaps my counterargument tends in the end toward a distinction without a difference. Either way, perhaps, God's love and freedom would still be the eternal, antecedent ground of all divine obedience and grace, while the Son of God's obedience and grace in the economy would be special determinations of God's love and freedom to all eternity.[3]

2. I have reformatted this material for easier reading. For several other examples where Barth reads God's relation to the economy back into an antecedent ground in God's eternal being—including mercy and patience—see Brian D. Asbill, *The Freedom of God for Us: Karl Barth's Doctrine of Divine Aseity* (London: T&T Clark, 2015), 119n78. Asbill massively confirms that the perfection of God's eternal being, for Barth, is prior to election.

3. For a similar line of questioning, see Paul D. Molnar, "The Obedience of the Son in the Theology of Karl Barth and of Thomas F. Torrance," *Scottish Journal of Theology* 67, no. 1 (February 2014): 50–69.

On the other hand, Barth's idea that the Son is eternally "subordinate" to the Father might be retrieved at least to this extent. Suppose that the Son, first in eternity but then also in time, is all that he is and has all that he has only through the renunciation of his own will.

Suppose that to all eternity, but then also in time, the Son knows and manifests his perfect deity precisely in perfect submission to his Father. Suppose that he always identifies his own will so completely with his Father's that the two are eternally one in a pattern of unity-in-distinction, but with the Father's will having primacy. In that case, the Son's free obedience in time would mirror his eternal relationship of perfect submission to his Father. Barth's doctrine of antecedence would be vindicated to that extent, even to the point of positing the Son's eternal (though functional) "subordination" to the Father as the ground of his incarnate obedience on earth. The Son would thus be no less "submissive" to the Father in the economy than he ever was and ever shall be to all eternity.[4]

On this interpretation there would be no unfitting "duality of willing" within the eternal Trinity between the Father and the Son. They would share the one indivisible essence (*ousia*) in which God's willing and being are identical, but they would do so in their own respective ways. The Son would partake fully of the Father's being and will precisely by receiving the former (his being) and by subjecting himself perfectly to the latter (his will). He would possess the very being and life of the Father through the eternal generation that constitutes him absolutely (not provisionally) for who he is. His will would be one and the same as the Father's, but he would receive it from the Father in the mode of perfect and eternal submission. His identity of will with the Father would be a oneness of differentiated unity. There would therefore be no "irresolvable aporiae" of two opposing or dichotomous divine wills in Barth's doctrine of the eternal Trinity.[5]

4. Cf. C. F. D. Moule, "The New Testament and the Doctrine of the Trinity," *Expository Times* 78 (1976): 16–20.

5. I am responding here to Thomas Joseph White, "Classical Christology after Schleiermacher and Barth: A Thomist Perspective," *Pro Ecclesia* 20 (2011): 229–63; on 246. Although Fr. White accepts the validity of the revisionist reading of Barth, he subjects it to devastating theological critique. His relatively legitimate protestations are one more reason why it is important to show that the revisionist reading of Barth is untenable. One might wonder, however, whether Fr. White's sweeping rejection of

Professor Nimmo's Argument in Retrospect

Having cited a passage that supported the "weak" (traditionalist) view (IV/2, 345), Professor Nimmo appeals to another, more lengthy passage (IV/1, 192–210) in support of his own "strong" (revisionist) position. A detailed analysis of that passage has shown, however, that it does not support the "strong" view. Not only is it entirely consonant with the passage cited from IV/2—so that there is no "contradiction" between them—but it provides compelling evidence for the view Professor Nimmo would reject.

It might be instructive at this point to inquire about what, at least in part, may have misled Professor Nimmo and other Barth-revisionists. It is clear that some of Barth's rhetoric in IV/1 is potentially misleading, in particular his use of the term "history." Although a careful reading makes it possible for Barth not to be misjudged, his peculiar use of the term "history" could lead the unwary reader astray.

In the course of IV/1 Barth uses the term in more than one sense but without always indicating what he is doing. He leaves it to the reader to puzzle out his different meanings by attending to the immediate context. His use of the term *history* is essentially twofold. On the one hand, he means something similar to what we would expect, while on the other, he signifies something we would not expect, namely, a "history" intrinsic to the eternal being of God as such. I propose to "disambiguate" Barth by designating his concept of God's eternal history as "history_1" and his concept of God's earthly history as "history_2."

A good example of the ambiguity appears at the outset of IV/1.[6] The phrase "God with us" is, Barth says, "a report about the being and life and act of God" (IV/1, 6). Is Barth here referring to God's being, life, and act *ad intra* or *ad extra*? Or is he perhaps referring to both at the same time? Could it be that "God's being, life, and act"

"duality" in favor of sheer "identity" can adequately differentiate the Son's will from the Father's within the eternal Trinity. Is it not a matter of one indivisible divine will in different hypostatic forms (as opposed to one undifferentiated divine will)? In other words, is Fr. White's conception of God's will sufficiently trinitarian?

6. Although IV/1, 192–210, and IV/1, 6–8, are not without their ambiguities, my interpretation of them satisfies the principle of charity (unlike revisionist readings).

ad intra are constituted by God's history with us *ad extra*, in other words, that $history_1$ (eternal) is constituted by $history_2$ (temporal)? Is Barth suggesting that God constitutes his eternal being in and through his "common history" with us (IV/1, 7)? If so, that would certainly count in support of the revisionist reading. It would give them a passage in their favor, one that confirmed their claim that the later Barth is not always consistent.

The phrase "God with us," Barth continues, "tells us that we ourselves are in the sphere of God." It tells us about "a history which God wills to share with us and therefore of an invasion of our history—indeed, of the real truth about our history as a history which is by him and from him and to him" (IV/1, 7). Again, is Barth assuming that this history that God shares with us is a history that "constitutes" his being, life, and act? Barth states,

> The divine being and life and act takes place with ours, and *it is only as the divine takes place that ours takes place*. To put it in the simplest way, what unites God and us human beings is that he does not will to be God without us, that he creates us rather to share with us and therefore with our being and life and act his own incomparable being and life and act, *that he does not allow his history to be his, and ours ours, but causes them to take place as a common history*. . . .
>
> The whole being and life of God is *an activity*, both in eternity and in worldly time, both in himself as Father, Son, and Holy Spirit, and in his relation to humankind and all creation. But what God does in himself and as the Creator and Governor of humankind is all aimed at the particular act in which it has its center and meaning. (IV/1, 7, rev.; italics added)

The "particular act" at which God eternally aims, according to Barth, is the covenant in which he is "God with us." What God does—not only in creation and providence, but also "in himself as Father, Son, and Holy Spirit"—is all said to be ordered to this goal (IV/1, 8). It seems that there is a single "eternal activity" in which God has his being, "both in himself and in the history of his acts in the world created by him" (IV/1, 8). In other words, there is one indivisible activity in which God subsists, and it would seem to embrace not only $history_1$ but also $history_2$.

How are these two histories (the temporal and the eternal) related here for Barth? Are they perhaps two sides of the same coin, two aspects of a single, symmetrical "common history"? Are they perhaps related by a pattern of "dialectical identity"?[7] From the textual evidence cited so far, it would be hard to say. It would even seem that the revisionists might be onto something.

If there is one history common to God and the creature, and if in this history God's being is in the process of self-actualization or even self-constitution, then revisionists like Professor Nimmo would appear to be correct. By historicizing the being of God, Barth would have abandoned "classical metaphysics" or "classical theism" in favor of an "actualistic ontology." He would be compelled to "historicize" (or perhaps even abandon) many of the attributes classically ascribed to God such as eternality, immutability, impassibility, simplicity, timelessness, and aseity. He would have to break with his earlier volumes in *Church Dogmatics* and also with much of what he says in his later volumes.

Despite what might seem to be the case so far, however, Barth does not actually move in this direction—not in this passage from the opening of IV/1, and not anywhere in his later theology. He always upholds his doctrine of antecedence and with it the relational terms of the "Chalcedonian pattern." Furthermore, although he modifies the attributes classically ascribed to God, he does not abandon them. Although he modifies them because of his "actualism" (understood as a motif, not as a system), he does not discard them, because he continues in some form to subscribe to a "perfect being" theology, as we will see.

Throughout his work Barth signals his doctrine of antecedence in various ways. He does so, for example, by using terms like "self-repetition" and "correspondence" but also by using related terms like "reflect" and "confirm." He especially emphasizes the divine antecedence when he resorts to the idea of an "antithesis" between divine and creaturely being, or of a "sharp distinction" between them. For Barth, divine and creaturely being "correspond" to one another in Christ. God's antecedent being in perfection and self-sufficiency,

7. For a definition of "dialectical identity," see chap. 1, n22.

however, is always presupposed as over against the fallenness, finitude, and neediness of creaturely life.

According to Barth, the gift of unity between divine and creaturely being occurs in and through the incarnate Son. At the opening of IV/1, the gift of unity is said to occur in the form of a "common history." It is a dynamic unity governed by the "grammar" of the Chalcedonian pattern. Divine history in itself (history_1) and divine history in relation to us (history_2) are related not only in inseparable unity ("without separation or division") but also in abiding distinction ("without confusion or change"). Moreover, because the gift of unity presupposes the triune God's antecedent eternal perfection, history_1 and history_2 are asymmetrically related. They are therefore irreversible and cannot be reduced to one another. Most especially, history_1 does not depend on history_2 and cannot be collapsed into it.

An example of how the later Barth uses the relational terms of Chalcedon to maintain the asymmetrical unity that he posits between the divine and the human in Christ can be seen in the following passage.

> As Jesus Christ lives, there takes place in him both divine [*schöperfiche*] actualization of being, yet also in and with it creaturely [*geschöpfliche*] actualization; divine and creaturely life together, without the transformation [*Verwandlung*] of the one into the other, the mixing [*Vermischung*] of the one with the other, or separation and division [*Trennung und Scheidung*] between them. (IV/3, 40, rev.)

The relational terms used here in IV/3 are obviously lifted from the Chalcedonian formula: "without separation (*Trennung*) or division (*Scheidung*)," "without confusion (*Verwandlung*) or mix (*Vermischung*)."[8]

8. Professor Nimmo is mistaken when he denies (against my work) that Barth commonly makes use of the grammar of the Chalcedonian pattern, as Barth does in this statement (IV/3, 40). Another clear example can be found in IV/2, where Barth employs the relational terms of Chalcedon (in the original Greek) to set forth the relationship between "justification" and "sanctification" (IV/2, 499–511). In III/2 an extensive list of paired terms appears that Barth suggests can be related (formally) according to the same scheme: soul and body, heaven and earth, justification and sanctification, gospel and law, faith and works, preaching and sacraments, doctrine and ethics, church and state (III/2, 343). This list is not exhaustive. Cf. Nimmo, "Karl

What prevents the divine and the human from being "mixed" or "transformed" into one another? As already noted, for Barth it is ultimately the divine "antecedence" understood in terms of the Trinity's eternally perfect being. According to Barth, God's trinitarian being is always actualized perfectly in itself. In eternity (history$_1$) it is a matter of "the perfect being of God himself" (II/2, 172). It is a matter of the dynamic "perfection in which this Father and this Son are one" (IV/1, 209). It is a matter of "the wealth of his perfections" in eternity, understood as God's spontaneous self-actualization, a superabundant wealth where God's inner life lacks nothing in itself (II/2, 121). In short, it is a matter of God's antecedent triune perfection to all eternity as a "dynamic and living" perfection "which needs no filling" (IV/1, 202, 201).

God's external manifestation in human history (history$_2$) is therefore always a matter of "self-repetition" (not self-constitution), while the relationship of this free outward self-repetition to God's inner life in eternity (history$_1$) is always one of "correspondence," analogy, or similarity-in-difference (not dialectical identity). The ideas of "self-repetition" and "correspondence" were first introduced in I/1 when Barth explained how he saw the economic Trinity as being related to the immanent Trinity. He then made regular use of them throughout his dogmatics. For Barth, history$_1$ (God's trinitarian history in himself) "repeats" itself *ad extra* in history$_2$ (God's history with us) so that history$_2$ always stands in "correspondence" (not dialectical identity) with history$_1$.

As has been true for Barth in one way or another ever since his second Romans commentary,[9] between history$_1$ and history$_2$—as well as, more generally, between divine being and creaturely being—there stands "an absolute (and infinitely qualitative) distinction" (*unendlichem qualitativem Unterschied*) (IV/2, 61). Divine and creaturely being can be defined only "in a sharp distinction [*nur scharf unterscheidend*], and even antithesis [*gegensätzlich*]" to one another (IV/2, 61).[10] The

Barth and the *concursus Dei*—A Chalcedonianism Too Far?," *International Journal of Systematic Theology* 9 (2007): 58–72.

9. Barth, *The Epistle to the Romans* (London: Oxford University Press, 1933 [German original, 1922]).

10. Although Professor Molnar has been roundly criticized in some quarters for using the phrase "sharp distinction" to differentiate the economic from the immanent Trinity in Barth, he is fully justified by Barth's usage here (IV/2, 61). See Paul D. Molnar,

antithesis between them—and therefore between history$_1$ and history$_2$—points to a relationship that is asymmetrical and irreversible. In this asymmetry, the eternal perfection of the divine being necessarily enjoys priority and precedence over the fallenness and finitude of creaturely being. History$_1$, in other words, necessarily enjoys absolute priority and precedence over God's involvement in history$_2$. The ontological divide between the two histories is bridged only by a miracle of sovereign grace. In self-repetition and correspondence, God establishes an irreversible relationship to the creature based entirely on the eternal perfection of his inner trinitarian life.[11]

> In the inner life of God, as the eternal essence of Father, Son, and Holy Ghost, the divine essence does not, of course, need any actualization. On the contrary, it is the creative ground of all other, i.e., all creaturely actualizations. Even as the divine essence of the Son, it did not need his incarnation, his existence as man . . . to become actual. As the divine essence of the Son, it is the predicate of the one God. And as the predicate of this Subject, it is not in any sense merely potential but in every sense actual. (IV/2, 113)

The idea of "correspondence" is therefore used to explain how history$_1$ and history$_2$ are related. "According to the witness of Holy Scripture—in *correspondence* with his triune being, and as indicated by the biblical concept of eternity—God is historical even in himself [history$_1$], and much more so in his relationship to the reality which is distinct from himself [history$_2$]" (IV/1, 112, italics added). In this passage the relationship between history$_1$ and history$_2$ is explicitly described as one of "correspondence." This is Barth's standard usage. It appears again, for example, when he writes: "It pleased God—and this is what *corresponds* outwardly to and reveals the inward divine being and event—himself to become man" (IV/1, 129, italics added).

Divine Freedom and the Doctrine of the Immanent Trinity: In Dialogue with Karl Barth and Contemporary Theology (London: T&T Clark, 2002), 33, 64, 70, 101, 235, etc.

11. For passages from volume IV where the ideas of "self-repetition" and/or "correspondence" reappear, see IV/1, 112, 129, 187–88, 203, 205; IV/2, 341–42, 345–46; IV/3, 47, 79–80. Revisionism is incorrect when it claims that in the later Barth these ideas have been eliminated.

We may now return to the opening pages of IV/1. There, as we have seen, Barth states that it is only as "the divine being, life and act" take place that ours takes place (IV/1, 7). Note, however, that he does not say the reverse. He does not say that it is only as our being, life, and act take place that the divine takes place. He does not say this because he does not hold to it. On the contrary, as he often insists, God's being, life, and act take place in some essential sense without us.

Barth emphasizes, however, that we are united with God by grace because he does not will to be God without us (IV/1, 7). Nevertheless, as he states repeatedly, God could have been God without us. The one activity in which God subsists in both $history_1$ and $history_2$ must therefore be seen as an activity that is internally differentiated. Through one divine activity, God subsists in the former ($history_1$) in a way that is noncontingent (or necessary) while he subsists in the latter ($history_2$) in a way that is contingent (or non-necessary). In short, God subsists perfectly in $history_1$ and through self-repetition in $history_2$. The act in which God has his being involves this internal distinction.

For Barth, God's being, life, and act in relation to humankind ($history_2$) "corresponds to the Godhead of God active and revealed in [Christ]" (IV/1, 129). God repeats himself outwardly in revelation and so corresponds to himself as he is in eternity. What God does outwardly "corresponds to and reveals the inward divine being and event." It is this inward trinitarian event, however, that "constitutes the divine being [*das das göttliche Sein ausmacht*]" (IV/1, 129). What Barth says here is definitive of his entire dogmatics. God's triune being is revealed in $history_2$ but constituted in $history_1$.

Another passage to which Professor Nimmo appeals also involves the idea of correspondence. When God humbles himself in the incarnation, according to Barth, "he does not do it apart from its basis in his own being, in his own inner life. He does not do it *without any correspondence* to, but as the miraculously consistent ultimate continuation [*wunderbar konsequenter letzter Fortsetzung*] of the history in which he is God" (IV/1, 203, rev.; italics added). $History_2$ is here described as in some sense a miraculous continuation of $history_1$, while $history_1$ for its part is said to be the basis of $history_2$. $History_2$ "continues" $history_1$, but only as it also "corresponds" to it. The idea of correspondence rules out the idea that God is constituting himself in history$_2$ as opposed to simply repeating himself in it.

Along with other revisionists, however, Professor Nimmo focuses on the "continuation" part of Barth's statement at the expense of its "correspondence" part. He thinks Barth is suggesting that temporal events in the covenant of grace are just as fundamental to God's being as the Father/Son relationship is in God's eternal life.[12] As is clear from the passage as a whole, however, temporal events are by no means "fundamental" in this way.

The eternal history in which God is God (history$_1$) is something perfect and sufficient in itself. It then forms the basis of God's external self-repetition in relation to us (history$_2$). In this secondary history *ad extra*, God corresponds to himself without needing to constitute himself because he is already constituted eternally as the Trinity. The movement of divine activity from history$_1$ to history$_2$ is thus a movement from inner trinitarian perfection to self-repetition and correspondence.

Failure to differentiate properly between history$_1$ and history$_2$ seems endemic to the argumentation of Barth-revisionists. They think that history$_2$ is at least as fundamental to the constitution of God's being as history$_1$ (if not more so). They fail to see that for Barth, whether early or late, history$_2$ always involves God's self-repetition (not his self-constitution), so that what takes place in history$_2$ stands in correspondence (not dialectical identity) with God's inner life in eternity as the Trinity (history$_1$). For the actually existing textual Barth, God's work *ad extra* is always based on the perfection of his trinitarian life in eternity. God's work *ad extra* repeats that inner life and corresponds to it without being fundamental to God's being.

Barth and Classical Theism

Although Barth's use of the term *history* in volume IV may sometimes be ambiguous, it is not self-contradictory. A plausible account based

12. Paul T. Nimmo, "Barth and the Election-Trinity Debate: A Pneumatological View," in *Trinity and Election in Contemporary Theology*, ed. Michael T. Dempsey (Grand Rapids: Eerdmans, 2011), 175.

on Barth's own statements of how his two main uses of the term (history$_1$ and history$_2$) are mutually coherent can be constructed. This account not only satisfies the principle of charity but also makes better sense of the whole range of Barth's statements than the proposition that he is inconsistent.

It remains to explain something of how Barth's actualism comes to bear on his appropriation of classical theism. Barth drank deeply from the wells of both Anselm and Hegel. Without following either of them slavishly, he owed a great deal to them both.[13] With Anselm, he adopted many of the divine predicates associated with classical theism. With Hegel, however, he stressed that God's inner being was dynamic and not static. The result, in effect, was a cross between the two. What Barth shared with Anselm was informed by elements reminiscent of Hegel, while what he had in common with Hegel was qualified by elements reminiscent of Anselm. Barth's use of these various elements needs to be brought into focus.[14]

According to Anselm, God's being must be conceived as perfect being. Divine perfection involved at least the following elements.

- *Aseity*. God exists through himself and not through dependence on anything other than himself. He is therefore self-existent and self-sufficient. (*Monologion* 3)
- *Simplicity*. God's being is not composed of parts. It is therefore indivisible. (*Proslogion* 18)
- *Immutability*. God neither comes into being nor passes away. He exists beyond all change, flux, and corruption. He is therefore immortal. (*Monologion* 18, 25)
- *Impassibility*. God's being is wholly active. Nothing can act upon him. He is therefore invulnerable to suffering. (*Proslogion* 8)
- *Timelessness*. God is timelessly eternal. Although his eternity embraces created time, created time does not belong to God's eternal being. (*Monologion* 20–22)

13. I believe this claim holds true even if Barth's knowledge of Hegel was not extensive.

14. I am engaged here primarily in conceptual analysis. I am not offering a genetic account of how Barth may have acquired views reminiscent of either Anselm or Hegel.

Like Anselm, Barth affirmed the perfection of God's being. "[God as revealed in Christ] did not and does not lack anything in himself" (IV/2, 133; cf. IV/1, 213; III/1, 69). "This God is self-sufficient. This God knows perfect beatitude in himself. He is not under any need or constraint" (IV/2, 346). When God "determines to co-exist with a reality distinct from himself," this decision takes place "in an inconceivably free overflowing of his goodness" (IV/2, 346). "God is One in the infinite fullness of his divine life" (IV/3, 158). For Barth, God's being is self-existent, self-sufficient, and perfect, lacking nothing in itself. For Barth as for Anselm there is no element of contingency in God.

Nevertheless, Barth strongly rejected certain aspects of "classical theism." He worried that in this theology "God was at bottom a supreme being with neither life, nor activity, nor history, in a neutrality which can never be moved or affected by anything" (IV/1, 112). The living God was not the God of philosophical theology, Barth insisted, not "a supreme being, which is accidentally the sum of all conceivable excellencies" (IV/1, 341). Barth wrote,

> According to this conception God is everything in the way of aseity, simplicity, immutability, infinity, etc., but he is not the living God, that is to say, he is not the God who lives in concrete decision. God lives in this sense only figuratively. It is not something which belongs to his proper and essential life, but only to his relationship with the world. Basically, then, it may only be "ascribed" to him, while it is believed that his true being and likewise his true Godhead are to be sought in the impassibility which is above and behind his living activity within the universe. (II/2, 79)

Here Barth seems to reject the kind of aseity, simplicity, immutability, and impassibility that we found in Anselm. Although Anselm might or might not be exempt from this critique, the God of classical theism in general, as Barth saw it, was lifeless, neutral, and aloof. It was not clear how this deity could become incarnate without ceasing to be God. The unity of the triune God had to be conceived along different lines. "It is a dynamic and living unity," Barth urged, "not a dead and static" unity (IV/1, 202).

At this point we can begin to see why Hegel appealed to Barth. His philosophy was centered, as Barth noted with approval, in the idea of God as event. In Hegel's philosophy, Barth writes,

> the key to everything . . . [is] that reason, truth, concept, mind, God himself are understood as an *event*, and, moreover, only as an event. They cease to be what they are as soon as the event, in which they are what they are, is thought of as interrupted, as soon as a state [of being] is thought of in its place. Essentially reason and all its synonyms are life, movement, process. God is God only in his divine action, revelation, creation, reconciliation, redemption; as an absolute act, as *actus purus*.[15]

What theology could learn from Hegel more than from Anselm or classical theism is that God is the living God. Nevertheless, Barth was not uncritical of Hegel.[16] The "weightiest" problem in his philosophy, Barth continued, is his "failure to recognize that God is free" (420). Hegel seemed to circumscribe God's freedom by making God dependent on the world. The living God, however, is in no way conditioned by the world. "[God] does not need the action of another to be who he is in reaction to it, nor the reaction of another to be who he is in his own action. [God] is not like Hegel's absolute spirit who can develop to a synthesis only in thesis and antithesis. He is actual in himself—the One who is originally and properly actual" (IV/2, 53–54).

The Hegelian dialectic, as Barth saw it, was logically vulnerable to fatal reversals. In this dialectic, he noted, "there can be all kinds of reversals between the higher and the lower, *prius* [the antecedent] and *posterius* [the subsequent], God and the creature" (III/3, 134). Barth was deeply concerned to uphold "the irreversibility of the relationship between God and humankind" (IV/2, 83). For that reason he developed a doctrine of antecedence that contained no element of subsequence, because any notion of divine subsequence inevitably opened the door to reversibility. God existed absolutely through himself and not in dependence on anything other than himself. God's

15. Barth, *Protestant Theology in the Nineteenth Century* (Valley Forge, PA: Judson Press, 1973), 398–99. Further references by page number are in the text.

16. Barth famously stated that he was "fond of doing a bit of 'Hegeling.'" But that did not prevent him, of course, from doing a bit of "Anselming" and "Calvining" as well, to invent two equally hideous terms. The point is that Barth's "Hegeling" should not be pushed too far. As to "Hegeling," he added: "I do it eclectically." See Eberhard Busch, *Karl Barth: His Life from Letters and Autobiographical Texts* (Philadelphia: Fortress, 1976), 387.

relationship to the world was therefore irreversible. Neither God nor the world could be collapsed into the other.

> Freedom is . . . more than the absence of limits, restrictions, or conditions. . . . But freedom in its positive and proper qualities means to be grounded in one's own being, to be determined and moved by oneself. This is the freedom of the divine life and love. In this positive freedom of his, God is also unlimited, unrestricted and unconditioned from without. (II/1, 301)

The absolute perfection of God's antecedent being aligned Barth with Anselm, while its event character aligned him with Hegel. It was not enough to affirm with Anselm that God's being must be conceived as *actus purus*. It had to be conceived as more than that. God's being was "*actus purus et singularis*" (II/1, 263). For Barth the singularity of the act in which God has his being was a singularity involving event, decision, and above all sovereign freedom.

With the proviso established by this living singularity, Barth found it possible (and necessary) to accept in modified form certain divine predications of classical theism.

- *Aseity*. "God himself and he alone is the principle and source from which [he is] all that he is . . . eternally . . . in the act of his existence as the living God" (IV/3, 80). "This God has no need of us. This God is self-sufficient. . . . He is not under any need or constraint" (IV/1, 346).
- *Simplicity*. "God is certainly simple," but not according to "the absolutized idea of simplicity" as found in classical theism (II/1, 450). "God in himself is not just simple, but in the simplicity of his essence he is threefold—the Father, the Son, and the Holy Ghost" (III/2, 218). Because his simplicity includes multiplicity in itself (II/1, 329), the living God is free to operate in multiple ways *ad extra* without ceasing to be perfectly indivisible in himself.
- *Immutability*. God's immutability means that "he is always the same in every change" (II/1, 496). "He is what he is continually and self-consistently" (II/1, 494). Although he partakes freely in the alteration of creation, he does so as the Lord, so that his

being and essence do not change along with creation. "He is what he is in eternal actuality. He never is it only potentially (not even in part)" (II/1, 494). Whatever God does *ad extra*, he does in accord with his antecedent being. His external works always correspond (*entsprechen*) to something "in his own essence" (II/1, 496). In all his external works he remains "rich in himself," never losing, altering, or contradicting himself (II/1, 495). God's immutability is "the constancy of his faithfulness to himself" as the triune God who loves in freedom (IV/1, 561). His constancy is both "ethical" and "ontological."

- *Impassibility*. "[God] is absolute, infinite, exalted, active, impassible, transcendent, but in all this he is the One who loves in freedom, the One who is free in his love, and therefore not his own prisoner. He is all this as the Lord, and in such a way that he embraces the opposites of these concepts even while he is superior to them" (IV/1, 187). Barth agrees with classical theism that nothing apart from or opposed to God can cause him to suffer. He goes beyond classical theism, however, in positing that God freely and sovereignly takes human suffering into his own being through his union with humankind in the humanity of the incarnate Son. In and through the mediation of Christ, God takes suffering and death into his own being in order to triumph over them by destroying them. The impassible God becomes passible by grace. He truly suffers in Christ—in his divine being, not just in his humanity—but in so doing he remains strong to prevail. Suffering and death are destroyed in the annihilating fire of God's love. In this radicalized form Barth affirms with Cyril and Gregory of Nazianzus the suffering of the impassible God.[17]

17. In espousing a form of theopaschism, Barth is perhaps even closer to Gregory of Nazianzus than he is to Cyril of Alexandria. For Cyril, see *The Theology of St. Cyril of Alexandria*, ed. Thomas G. Weinandy and Daniel A. Keating (London: Continuum, 2003), 48–52. For Gregory, see Christopher A. Beeley, *Gregory of Nazianzus on the Trinity and the Knowledge of God* (Oxford: Oxford University Press, 2008), 138–39, 142. For Gregory perhaps even more than for Cyril, suffering and death enter into the divine life through the divine-human Christ, who is understood as a single subject, only for them to be destroyed there, as through fire. This is the essence of Barth's view as well.

- *Timelessness*. Although created time does not belong to God's eternal being, his being includes its own unique form of temporality. This unique time is "the [eternal] form of the divine being in its triunity." It is "a movement which does not signify the passing away of anything, a succession which in itself is also beginning and end" (II/1, 615). Without this inner eternal temporality, God as triune would not be the living God in himself (II/1, 638–39).[18]

These aspects or "perfections" of the divine being are not the same as those in classical theism because they are all qualified by God's sovereign freedom as the freedom of his love. The God who is self-sufficient is free in love to make himself needy for our sakes. The God whose being is indivisible is free in love to repeat himself in the flux of time as the triune God he is to all eternity. The God who is immutable is free in love to embrace temporal change without losing his essential constancy as the triune God. The God who is impassible is free in love to make the sufferings of the world his own without ceasing to be impassible in himself. Finally, the God whose timeless being includes a special temporality of its own is free in love to repeat in the economy the trinitarian history that he is eternally in himself.

The living God "embraces the opposites of [his divine predications] even while he is superior to them" (IV/1, 187). He acts as their Lord even while subjecting himself to them (IV/1, 185). He is free to enter fully into finitude, suffering, and death while persevering in their midst and prevailing over them. This exercise of God's freedom for the sake of his love is a manifestation of his true deity, not a contradiction of it.[19]

Barth does not abandon his "perfect being" theology for the sake of his "actualism." On the contrary, he incorporates his actualism into his perfect-being theology. Actualism is developed as an inner aspect of God's perfect being. It is a technical way of affirming that God in

18. The eternal temporality of God, as explained in II/1, correlates with the eternal historicity of the Trinity (history$_1$), as developed in IV/1. This line of continuity suggests once again that although there were significant developments in Barth after II/2, there were no radical breaks. It also suggests why history$_1$ cannot be collapsed into history$_2$.

19. This remarkable emphasis on God's sovereign freedom might be regarded as the "Calvinistic" moment in Barth's theology.

his perfection is the living God. God does not lack anything in himself, nor does he become the living God only in relation to the world. God is already the living God—Father, Son, and Holy Spirit—in and for himself to all eternity. In this way Barth incorporates "Anselmian" and "Hegelian" moments into his theology. He actualizes the divine perfections while maintaining their absolute, self-sufficient antecedence.

Immediately upon the heels of the lengthy passage (IV/1, 192–210) that Professor Nimmo thinks would support his position, Barth strongly reasserts the "Anselmian" moment in his theology.

> Nothing would be lacking in his inward being as God in glory, as the Father, Son, and Holy Spirit, as the One who loves in freedom, if he did not show himself to the world, if he allowed it to complete its course to nothingness: just as nothing would be lacking to his glory if he had refrained from giving it being when he created it out of nothing. (IV/1, 213, rev.)

> For himself he did not need that he and his glory should be revealed and confessed in the world and by us. He might have been content with his own knowledge of himself, just as he might have been content earlier with his being as God in glory, not needing the being of the creature and its co-existence with him, not being under any necessity to be its Creator. (IV/1, 212)

> The great and self-sufficient God wills to be *also* the Savior of the world. . . . *Deus pro nobis* is something which he did not have to be or become, but which, according to this fact, he was and is and will be—the God who acts as our God, who did not regard it as too mean a thing, but gave himself fully and seriously to self-determination as the God of the needy. (IV/1, 214, italics added)

These "Anselmian" statements are then followed by a passage whose flavor is more "Hegelian."

> The way of his humiliation is simply the way which leads him to us, the way on which he draws near to us and becomes one of us. And this means first that the mortal peril in which man stands becomes and is his peril, the need of man his need. The Son of God exists with man and as man in this fallen and perishing state. We should be explaining the incarnation docetically and therefore explaining it away if we did

> not put it like this, if we tried to limit in any way the solidarity with the cosmos which God accepted in Jesus Christ. We have already said that in this event God allows the world and humanity to take part in the history of the inner life of his Godhead, in the movement in which from and to all eternity he is Father, Son, and Holy Spirit, and therefore the one true God. But this participation of the world in the being of God implies necessarily his participating in the being of the world, and therefore that his being, his history, is played out as world-history and therefore under the affliction and peril of all world-history [*unter der ganzen Belastung, in der ganzen Gefahr aller Weltgeschichte*]. (IV/1, 215)

The God whose being is self-sufficient to all eternity is free to become flesh in Jesus Christ. He is free to draw near to us and become one of us. In Christ he takes our mortal peril to himself (to his own being) and makes it his own (as mediated through Christ). His solidarity with us knows no bounds. At the same time, in and through the mediation of Christ, he gives us a share in his own eternal blessedness. In and through Christ, he allows the world and humanity to take part (indirectly) in the history of the inner life of his Godhead. Through his self-repetition in history, he draws the world and humanity into the movement in which he is Father, Son, and Holy Spirit antecedently—from and to all eternity.

As God in Christ graciously participates in the world's being, the world gains a share in his eternal being. His eternal being is "played out" (*sich abspielt*: takes place, unfolds) as world history, with all the affliction and peril that history involves. God gives himself without losing himself in order that all things might be restored to himself—in and through Christ. What God is in eternity he reiterates and complicates in time so that what exists in time might be made new through the grace of participation in the beatitude of his eternal life.

This striking conjunction of absolute perfection with extreme vulnerability is mysterious, and no nonparadoxical way of stating it will do. Any attempt to resolve the tension—either in the "Anselmian" direction of perfection or else in the "Hegelian" direction of actualism—would lose one of the essential elements of Barth's theology. For Barth, the eternal God becomes fully actualized in the economy without ceasing to be perfectly actualized in eternity (antecedently, in his infinite qualitative difference). The perfect being of God subjects itself fully to suffering and death for the sake of the world without ceasing to be perfect and unimpaired in itself. God's eternal history is fully played out and repeated as world history with all its peril and affliction—according to the pattern of an asymmetrical unity-in-distinction.

In order to say what he thinks must be said, Barth needs both the "Anselmian" and the "Hegelian" moments—and neither one without the other. For Barth, there is no Anselmian moment without the Hegelian and no Hegelian moment without the Anselmian. Any attempt to commandeer the Hegelian moment at the expense of the Anselmian moment would lead only to a defective reading of Barth, who embraces them both while keeping them in unresolved tension.

5

Revisionism Scaled Back

A Partial Dissent

One of the outstanding works of recent Barth scholarship is *The Humanity of Christ: Christology in Karl Barth's Church Dogmatics* by Paul Dafydd Jones.[1] Perhaps the most sophisticated of the revisionists, Professor Jones aligns himself with Barth-revisionism while discarding many of its themes. Gone is the abstractly deduced picture of Barth, the penchant for accusing Barth of self-contradiction, and the black-and-white mode of reasoning—all of which detract from other revisionist efforts. Also abandoned is the attempt to force Barth into the Procrustean bed of an "actualistic ontology." These are welcome advances. Professor Jones is all the more formidable as an interpreter for having left these themes behind.

Above all, Professor Jones distances himself from the allegation, which I have shown above to be false, that in II/2 Barth turned the Trinity into a consequence of pretemporal election. He recognizes that for Barth the Trinity is always election's presupposition, not its

1. Paul Dafydd Jones, *The Humanity of Christ: Christology in Karl Barth's Church Dogmatics* (London: T&T Clark, 2008). Pages numbers hereafter are cited in the text.

product. He thereby abandons what is probably revisionism's most unfortunate idea. Nevertheless, Professor Jones retains a softer version of what I have called "the doctrine of subsequence." Although I think his version of this idea is untenable as it stands, I also believe that much of it can be retrieved. That cannot be done, however, without careful conceptual analysis—more careful than that of which Professor Jones avails himself.

His argument begins innocently enough before taking a regrettable turn. He states that for Barth, God's pretemporal decision of election "entails an event of divine self-qualification; . . . God decides, freely, that the economic elective activity of the Son, realized by way of his union with a contingent human being, should prove eternally determinative for God's second way of being" (61). The operative terms in this statement are *divine self-qualification* and *eternally determinative*. They mean that when God acts in pretemporal election, his decision has eternal consequences for his way of being (τρόπος ὑπάρξεως) as the eternal Son.

As thus stated, this idea is not in dispute between the traditionalists and the revisionists. Both camps would agree that for Barth, God determines himself in pretemporal election, and that when God does so, it has far-reaching consequences not only for humankind but also for God himself.

In a rather less cautious vein, however, Professor Jones also asserts that Christ's divinity is "altered by the hypostatic union" (37), that the Son's actions in the economy have "immanent ramifications" (40), and that God's decision to become incarnate involves him in "ontological complications" (41). These statements, although perhaps not entirely wrong, represent Professor Jones's most fundamental intuition, namely, that for Barth the incarnation does not leave God's eternal being unaffected. With the addition of some careful qualifications, these statements would also be defensible, in a pinch, from a traditionalist point of view.

The following explanation, however, indicates the point at which things start to go wrong.

> I am using, and will continue to use, a whole cluster of terms—self-determination, self-qualification, self-constitution, self-conditioning,

> even self-transformation to describe this aspect of Barth's doctrine of God. The reason for this cluster is to ensure that analysis does not get bogged down in semantic disputes but rather focuses directly on the radical way in which God qua Son takes on an identity inclusive of the concrete life of Jesus Christ. (61n)

By opting for terminological imprecision, Professor Jones effectively grants himself license to indulge in rhetorical extravagance. He muddies the waters at precisely the point where the revisionists and the traditionalists are in dispute. To Barth, terms like *self-determination* and *self-qualification* would not mean the same as very different terms like *self-constitution* and *self-transformation*.

Professor Jones treats these important differences with insouciance. Nevertheless, although his rhetoric can be excessive, it can also be ambiguous. If the rhetorical excess is trimmed back, and if the ambiguities are resolved in a particular direction, the doctrine of subsequence that Professor Jones wants to advance can be retrieved from a traditionalist point of view.

To frame the issues, we might say that for Barth the doctrine of God involves at least three main elements: (1) eternal constituents, (2) essential predications, and (3) material determinations. What Professor Jones tends to obscure is that element (3)—the divine self-determination expressed in election and incarnation—in no way alters the essential constitution of elements (1) and (2). God's self-determination for Barth always presupposes the perfection of these two main elements. It adds a series of differentiae to them insofar as they are already constituted. God freely gives himself a new set of material determinations that distinguish his being relative to what it was (logically and ontologically) before. Elements (1) and (2), however, would be *essentially* what they are without these added differentiae, and, equally important, they remain *essentially* what they were even after these differentiae are added to them.[2]

(1) *Eternal constituents*. For Barth God is eternally constituted as the Holy Trinity through a primordial act in which nature and

2. I am using the term *differentiae* not to distinguish genus and species (as in Aristotle) but to distinguish the triune God with the properties he acquired through the incarnation from the triune God as he would be without them.

will are inseparably one (I/1, 435). God's act of self-determination in election and incarnation, on the other hand, always presupposes God's prior, primordial identity as the Trinity. Note that the idea of "self-determination" involves not *whether* God is triune but rather *how* God decides to be triune. God determines to be triune in a way that takes human neediness into account. As Barth never tires of saying, God determines not to be God without us—which is very different from saying that God determines to "constitute" himself in and through his relationship to us.

(2) *Essential predications*. Much the same line of thinking applies to God's essential predications or perfections. The triune God is already constituted in and of himself as eternal, simple, impassible, immutable, and so on. These predications need to be defined in such a way that they can be determined materially by election and incarnation—which is exactly how Barth defines them. Their constitution is such that God can even enter into their apparent opposites without incurring either self-contradiction or basic alteration. These essential predications include an innate and infinite resourcefulness that allows God to determine himself in a radical and startling way. The richness of these predications is prior to election and incarnation, not subsequent to them.

We could then say that for Barth, God has two sorts of defining properties: noncontingent and contingent (i.e., necessary and non-necessary).[3] The burden of Professor Jones's argument seems to be that for Barth God's non-necessary but freely chosen properties make a material difference for God. If that is what he means, I think he is correct.

What his rhetoric obscures, however, is the distinction between these two sorts of properties. He sometimes writes as if God's contingent properties serve to "transform" his noncontingent properties (like eternality, simplicity, impassibility, and immutability) into something essentially other than they were before. That is his questionable doctrine of subsequence—or at least the impression he leaves by his unguarded rhetoric. At the point where other revisionists would posit

3. I am using the term *properties* loosely here to mean "features" or "characteristics." Barth allows for this usage as seen in his appeal to *propria* and *proprietates* at IV/2, 75.

divine *self-constitution* through election and incarnation, Professor Jones posits divine *self-transformation* instead. This is a variation on an unfortunate theme.

By contrast, the traditionalists would insist that for Barth a divine property is contingent if God could have been God without it. A contingent property is thus one whose existence or nonexistence for God is equally possible. A property is also contingent if its absence would entail no self-contradiction for God and if its presence would entail no essential alteration.

(3) *Material determinations*. In these ways election and incarnation involve contingent divine properties. Properties like divine suffering, for example, are contingent. God did not have to choose them. Their existence or nonexistence is equally possible for him. Their absence would imply no self-contradiction for him, and their presence no essential alteration. God could have been God without them, and he remains *essentially* the same upon choosing them.

Despite being non-necessary, these properties are freely chosen by God. Once chosen, they contribute to the definition of God's identity. Nevertheless, they do not transform God's basic, noncontingent properties into something essentially other than they were before. God's noncontingent properties are already so constituted that his contingent properties can be added to them without effecting either self-contradiction or essential transformation. This is Barth's doctrine of antecedence according to traditionalist understanding.

Traditionalists can therefore agree with Professor Jones to a certain extent. Once chosen, God's contingent properties do indeed define his identity in a way that makes a difference for him. God will never be another than the One incarnate in Jesus Christ, who took suffering, sin, and death into his divine being in order to destroy them.

For Barth, God's contingent properties are thus defining properties, and they make a difference for the way God has chosen to be himself as the triune God. But the difference they make is by addition and self-qualification, not by essential transformation. God's contingent properties represent the way in which he actualizes himself *ad extra* without losing or essentially altering himself. By becoming human in Jesus Christ, God adds to himself a series of differentiae without changing his formal constitution.

For Barth, God's subsequent, post-incarnational identity is an actualization, qualification, revelation, and confirmation of his antecedent, primordial attributes, not a transmutation of them into something else. God's "eternal constituents" (his identity as the Trinity) and "essential predications" (like eternality, simplicity, impassibility, and immutability) remain what they always were. They are simply actualized by dint of sovereign self-determination in a radical and startling way.

God's subsequent reality (after election and incarnation) does not represent a transition from potentiality to actuality. Nor does it represent any kind of fundamental self-transformation. It is rather the self-determination *ad extra* of the triune God, who remains essentially one and the same. By entering into union with Jesus of Nazareth, the triune God reiterates himself *ad extra* and augments himself *ad intra* in a way that is at once absolutely constant and yet also radically new.

Like other revisionists, Professor Jones errs by emphasizing the newness at the expense of the constancy.[4] He does so especially when claiming, as he repeatedly does, that election and incarnation entail something so new for God as to effect his ontological "self-transformation." Although (happily) this is not the only register in which Professor Jones chooses to speak, here are some examples of his argument at its most insupportable.

According to Professor Jones, few modern theologians were as committed as Barth to "a reconstructive agenda of such radical proportions" (2). He contends that for Barth, pretemporal election effects in God a "christic self-transformation" (105). It "transforms God's eternal being" (65). It has "an impact on God's being as such" (67). It "freely transforms God's immanent being" (103). "God in fact transforms God's being" (115). God undergoes "an eternal ontological transformation" (207). He transforms himself eternally (248).

In what does this "eternal ontological transformation" supposedly consist? Apparently it is thought that for Barth, God somehow historicizes his eternal being. "God decides to shape [his] eternal life in temporal terms" (191). "The contingent history of [Jesus] . . . supplies the unchanging content of God's life qua Son" (149). "The

4. The equal and opposite error would be finding little more to appreciate throughout Barth than "the same dull thud." See Paul McGlasson, *Jesus and Judas: Biblical Exegesis in Barth* (Atlanta: Scholars Press, 1991), 45.

economy . . . is drawn into, and ramifies within, the eternal life of God" (67). God's being thereby takes on "an inherently diachronic identity, bound to the irreducibly contingent life of Jesus Christ" (193). "Christ's concrete existence becomes eternally constitutive of God's second way of being. So much is epitomized by the fine but important distinction between God's *souveräne Güte* and God's *eminenter Gnade*" (248).

All this is quite confused, and it's hard to know where to begin. Let's start with something simple. According to Professor Jones, Barth operates with a "distinction between 'sovereign' and 'eminent' grace" (95). "Eminent" grace is thought to be that by which God transforms (or historicizes) his eternal, immanent being. However, not only is there no such "transformation" in Barth, as we will see, but there is also no such thing as *eminent grace*. What Barth says in the passage from which Professor Jones extracts this unheard-of term is that in election God exercises his grace *in eminenter Weise*—that is, "in an eminent way" (II/2, 121). Note that the phrase is adverbial, not adjectival. It does not modify the noun but modifies the verb. Barth's point is that in election, God's grace is exercised in an outstanding way. This misreading (which is used to support the erroneous claim of divine "self-transformation") does not inspire confidence.[5]

Nor is it reassuring to see the immanent history of the eternal Trinity absorbed into the earthly history of Jesus (or vice versa). Like other revisionists, Professor Jones fails to maintain a proper distinction between what has already been discussed at length as "history$_1$" and "history$_2$." He does not grasp their asymmetrical unity-in-distinction. He misses the way in which the concepts of "overflowing," "correspondence," and "repetition" function for Barth at this point. He is oblivious to Barth's clear use of Chalcedon to establish the grammar by which these two "histories" (eternal and temporal) are inseparably related while also remaining abidingly distinct. He stresses their oneness but obscures their distinction.

Indeed, if Professor Jones had been more sensitive to how Barth actually uses the Chalcedonian pattern, his rhetoric about divine

5. Barth, who vigorously insists that God's grace is indivisible, has an allergic reaction against divvying grace up into different kinds. See IV/1, 84–87. The term *eminente Gnade* is nowhere to be found in *Kirchliche Dogmatik*.

"self-transformation" might have been less freewheeling. *Verwandlung*, the usual German word for *transformation*, is something that Barth always ruled out. The incarnation effects no "mixture" (*Mischgebilde*) of divine and human "forms" (*Gestalten*) into a hybrid third (*verschmelzenden Dritte*) (IV/1, 136)—not in the person of Christ and not in the immanent Trinity.

> When . . . the later [Chalcedonian] Christology ruled out any "confusion" [*Vermischung*] or "transformation" [*Verwandlung*] of the two "natures," the one into the other and therefore into a third, the move was entirely justified. (IV/1, 136, rev.)

> The first part of the Chalcedonian definition is relevant in this connection with its safeguarding against the excesses of Alexandrian theology. One and the same Christ, the only-begotten Son and Lord, is to be confessed in two natures ἀσυγχύτως (*inconfuse*) and ἀτρέπτως (*immutabiliter*), and therefore without any idea of a commixture [*Vermischung*] of the two or a transformation [*Verwandlung*] of the one into the other. (IV/2, 63, rev.)

> As Jesus Christ lives, there takes place in him both divine actualisation of being, yet also in and with it creaturely actualisation; divine and creaturely life together, without the transformation [*Verwandlung*] of the one into the other, the admixture [*Vermischung*] of the one with the other, or separation or division between them. This is how Jesus Christ is seen and attested in Scripture. (IV/3, 40, rev.)

> The correspondence [*Entsprechung*] which alone can be considered in this connection cannot and will not mean abolition of "the infinite qualitative difference" between God and man. It is a question of responsibility and therefore of a correspondence in which God and man are in clear and inflexible antithesis. It is [not] a question . . . of mixing [*Vermischung*] or transforming [*Verwandlung*] the human form into the divine form. (II/2, 577, rev.)

The same result appears if we turn to the related word *Veränderung*.

> God is always God even in his humiliation. The divine being [*Das göttliche Wesen*] does not suffer any change [*Veränderung*], any diminution, any transformation [*Verwandlung*] into something else, any admixture [*Vermischung*] with something else, let alone any cessation. The deity of Christ [*Die Gottheit Christi*] is the one unaltered [*unveränderte*]

> because unalterable [*unveränderliche*] deity of God [*Gottheit Gottes*]. Any subtraction or weakening of it would at once throw doubt upon the atonement made in him. He humbled himself, but he did not do it by ceasing to be who he is. He went into a strange land, but even there, and especially there, he never became a stranger to himself. (IV/1, 179–80)[6]

Professor Jones is correct when he states that Barth "did not draw especial attention to his innovative thinking about God's self-transformation" (90). The reason Barth did not draw "especial attention" to it, however, is that he did not teach it. In fact he explicitly denied it. In accord with Chalcedon, he was always adamantly opposed to any "transformation" (*Verwandlung*) of the divine into the human, of the human into the divine, or even (as Professor Jones apparently believes) of the divine by admixture (*Vermischung*) with the human. The union of Jesus with the eternal Son by virtue of pretemporal election effects in God no "eternal ontological transformation."

What exactly does Professor Jones have in mind with all his unfortunate talk about "divine self-transformation"? He gives us this clue. "'Transform' in the sense that this loving action lends God an identity, the form of which is other than that which God possesses pre-temporally and the content of which is other than the ontological simplicity characteristic of God's pre-temporal, human-less, triune interrelating" (89).

Professor Jones is correct to observe that the contingent properties God adopts in the incarnation lend him a new "identity." He is also correct that this identity differentiates God from what he would otherwise have been if he had not adopted these properties. What he fails to see, however, is that for Barth everything depends on God's being able to adopt these incarnational properties without undergoing anything so drastic as an "eternal ontological transformation." He fails to see that what he misconstrues as a matter of subsequence is actually developed in Barth as a function of the divine antecedence. He fails to realize that for Barth everything depends on seeing God's prior essential predications (like eternality, simplicity, impassibility, and immutability) as capable of taking on a new configuration or "identity" without being fundamentally transformed. Adding contingent properties (or differentiae) to these predications, no matter

6. It would be tedious to pursue this sort of documentation any further.

how radically and mysteriously, is not the same as subjecting them to an eternal ontological transformation.

In short, the Son of God "adds human essence to his divine essence" (IV/2, 66) while still remaining the "one unchangeably true God" (IV/2, 41). His incarnation "does not remove or alter either the divine essence . . . or the human essence" (IV/2, 51). "The divine essence and the human essence are indivisibly united" (IV/2, 64) even as their "absolute (and infinitely qualitative) distinction" remains (IV/2, 61). Most especially, the Son enters into the *assumptio carnis* without "any diminution or alteration of his Godhead" (IV/1, 180). His Godhead remains exactly what it was "with all the perfections proper to it" (IV/2, 65). As Augustine wrote, "In taking the form of a servant, he did not lose the form of God. The form of a servant came, but the form of God did not leave" (as cited in IV/1, 180; Latin translated).

Barth on Chalcedon and Divine Suffering

Barth is very bold in his argument that the incarnation involves God in suffering. How can the impassible God suffer without transforming himself? That is the deepest question raised by Professor Jones's account.[7] Barth contends not only that the incarnate Son suffers but also that there is an element of truth in "patripassionism," the idea—generally regarded as heretical—that the Father suffers along with the Son. In effect Barth extends the Augustinian principle *opera trinitatis ad extra sunt indivisa*—the external works of the Trinity are indivisible—to include divine suffering. If the Sythian monks were correct in 513 (as vindicated at the Fifth Ecumenical Council in 553) that *unus ex trinitate passus est* (one of the Trinity suffered in the flesh), then in some sense it would also be true to say that *passionis trinitatis ad extra sunt indivisa*—the external sufferings of the Trinity are indivisible.[8]

The purpose of this section is to show how Barth could posit that divine suffering occurred in Christ without entangling God in

7. He does not explore this question at any length. I will consider his statements at a later point.

8. This reference to the Sythian monks, the Fifth Ecumenical Council, and the reformulation of the Augustinian principle are my own. They do not appear in Barth, though I think they are consistent with his views.

an eternal divine transformation. In particular, how did Barth think that divine suffering was related to divine impassibility? Impassibility was one of the basic predications that differentiated Jesus Christ's true deity (*vere Deus*) from his true humanity (*vere homo*). Divine suffering, on the other hand, was a contingent property resulting from Barth's unitive view of the incarnation. Reminiscent of Gregory of Nazianzus and Cyril of Alexandria, Barth maintained that through the incarnation of the eternal Son, God suffered in his divine nature without ceasing to be essentially impassible. God suffered in one sense without ceasing to be impassible in another.

Barth does not hesitate to ascribe suffering and death to God himself. The Pauline statement "God was in Christ" (2 Cor. 5:19 KJV) means, he suggests, "that in the man Jesus, God himself was at work, speaking and acting and suffering and going to his death" (IV/1, 301). It is God himself who suffers, "who takes the place of the former sufferers and allows the bitterness of their suffering to fall upon himself" (IV/1, 175). God's suffering occurs through the incarnation. "In Jesus Christ God himself . . . has suffered what it befell this man to suffer to the bitter end" (IV/3, 414). In the passion and death of Jesus, what took place was "the final depth of the self-humiliation of God" (IV/2, 116). "[Jesus] really suffered our distress as the distress in the heart of God himself" (II/1, 402).

God's entry into suffering and death is seen as grounded in pretemporal election.

> If we would know what it was that God elected for himself when he elected fellowship with humankind, then we can answer only that he elected our rejection. He made it his own. He bore it and suffered it with all its most bitter consequences. For the sake of this choice and for the sake of humankind, he hazarded himself wholly and utterly. He elected our suffering. . . . He elected it as his own suffering. This is the extent to which his election is an election of grace, an election of love, an election to give himself, an election to empty and abase himself for the sake of the elect. (II/2, 164–65, rev.)

God elected to suffer and die for us on the cross that we might be spared from our self-imposed ruin and be reconciled to him. "In this suffering and dying of God himself in his Son, there took place the reconciliation [of the world] with God" (IV/1, 250–51). God's suffering and death were vicarious. "He suffered as our Representative the death which we had merited, dying in our place" (IV/2, 301). He bore the judgment that would otherwise have befallen us. "There takes place here the redemptive judgment of God on all humanity. To fulfill this judgment he took the place of all humanity, he took their place as sinners. . . . On that one day of [God's] suffering [in Christ], there took place the comprehensive turning in the history of all creation—with all that this involves" (IV/1, 247, rev.).

Through the extremity of suffering and death, God seeks to restore us to fellowship with himself. Taking our dreadful plight of sin and death to himself in Christ, he gives us the gift of his righteousness and life.

> He so enters into fellowship with [the fallen creature], and into so complete a fellowship, that he himself, God, takes his place, to suffer for him in it what he [the creature] had to suffer, to make good for him the evil he had done, so that he [the human creature], in turn, may take God's place, that he, the sinner, may be clothed with God's holiness and righteousness and therefore be truly holy and righteous. (II/1, 663)

> Because [God in Christ] bears [our sins], the suffering and punishment for them are lifted from us, and our own suffering can be only a reminiscence of his. As he takes to himself our sin and guilt in his Son, we are freed from the necessity of seeing and suffering and lamenting except as his and by faith in him, i.e., except as a burden of sin and guilt which is lifted from us by him. It remains for us only to be the sinners whose place he has taken and who must therefore really have their life in him. (II/1, 374)

God suffers in his assumed humanity, but beyond that he is also affected in his eternal being. His self-humiliation involves the obedience of the Son but also, at the same time, the mercy of the Father. The Father is the Father of mercies who exists, like the Son, in a way that is at once exalted and yet also lowly.

> For what is represented and reflected in the humiliation of God is the mercy of the Father in which he too is not merely exalted but lowly with his Son, allowing himself to be so affected by the misery of the creature, of man, that to save it, to endow it with eternal life, he does

not count it too high a cost to give and send his Son, to elect him to take our place as the Rejected, and therefore to abase him. (IV/2, 357)

It would be a mistake to suppose that God suffers only in the economy but not also in eternity, only in the Son but not also in the Father, only in the incarnation but not also in the divine essence. Barth's single-subject Christology is a unitive Christology. There is no shadow of Nestorianism in his understanding of divine suffering. Although divine and human essence remain abidingly distinct in Christ, they are inseparably one in his passion and death. As God suffers "in the person of his own Son," he suffers also "in his fatherly heart" (IV/3, 414–15).

It is not at all the case that God has no part in the suffering of Jesus Christ even in his mode of being as the Father. No, there is a *particula veri* in the teaching of the early Patripassians. This is that primarily it is God the Father who suffers in the offering and sending of his Son, in his abasement. The suffering is not his own, but the alien suffering of the creature, of man, which he takes to himself in him. But he does suffer it in the humiliation of his Son with a depth with which it never was or will be suffered by any human being—apart from the One who is his Son. . . . This fatherly fellow-suffering of God is the mystery, the basis, of the humiliation of his Son; the truth of that which takes place historically in his crucifixion. (IV/2, 357, rev.)

The suffering and death that God takes into himself in Christ is something entirely voluntary. "From all eternity he willed to suffer for us" (II/2, 165). "It is his own will which is done, his own plan and decision which is executed" (IV/1, 195). "It becomes the work of God himself, as God gives himself to this most dreadful of all foreign spheres" (IV/1, 175). Suffering is not imposed on him from without. "God finds no suffering in himself. And no cause outside God can cause him suffering if he does not will it so" (II/1, 370). When entering into suffering and death, God does so in sovereign freedom.

God's free decision to accept suffering and death is not something improper. It manifests not a defect in his deity but the plenitude of his eternal perfection.

> God's being consists in the fact that he is the One who loves in freedom. In this he is the perfect being: the being which is itself perfection and so the standard of all perfection; the being, that is, which is self-sufficient and thus adequate to meet every real need; the being which suffers no lack in itself and by its very essence fills every real lack. Such a being is God. (II/1, 322)

God freely determines his perfect being as a being in compassion. "God does not have to, but he can, take to himself the suffering of another" (II/1, 375). His entry into suffering is not improper for him. "In doing so . . . he does what corresponds to his worth" (II/1, 375). By taking on our suffering in order to remove it, God expresses the true depths of his Godhead. "As the One who loves in sovereign freedom, he activates and proves his Godhead—as opposed to discarding it—by giving himself to humanity in humiliation and suffering" (IV/1, 134, rev.).

True Godhead is not incapable of existing in the form of meekness. On the contrary, it is fully manifest in the form of meekness.[9] "True Godhead in the New Testament exists in the absolute freedom of love—as something high and almighty and eternal and righteous and glorious—and it does this not also but precisely in meekness" (IV/1, 191, rev.). God "is the One who, concretely in his being as human, activates and reveals himself as divinely free" (IV/1, 134, rev.). "He can be and wills to be true God not only in the height but also in the depth—in the depth of human creatureliness, sinfulness and mortality" (IV/1, 134). God manifests his greatness in the form of self-humiliation.

God's free decision to accept suffering, even to the point of death on a cross, arises from the depths of his freedom and love.

> God is moved and stirred, yet not like ourselves in powerlessness, but in his own free power, in his innermost being: moved and touched by himself, i.e., open, ready, inclined (*propensus*) to compassion with another's suffering and therefore to assistance, impelled to take the

9. Barth cites Gregory of Nyssa favorably in this regard. "So far as I know Gregory of Nyssa (*Or. Cat.* 24) was the only one of the Church fathers expressly to mention that the descent to humility which took place in the incarnation . . . is not only not excluded by the divine nature but signifies its greatest glory" (IV/2, 192).

initiative to relieve this distress. It can be only a question of compassion, free sympathy, with another's suffering. (II/1, 370)

God's compassion is what leads him to the cross. Moreover, his suffering is not only voluntary, befitting, and compassionate. It is also effectual. To see why, according to Barth, three aspects need to be considered: (1) the human death of Jesus, (2) the participation of the eternal Son in that death, and (3) its mediation into the life of God. As God takes our death into his life, it is eternally destroyed—along with the sin that led to it.

Barth is emphatic that sin has no right to exist. In the death of Christ God has intervened to destroy it. "For [the wrong of sin] is an outrage and abomination to God. It has to perish. The right of God confronts it with such majesty. It cannot exist before it. It is taken and burnt up and destroyed by the life of God like dry wood by the fire" (IV/1, 539). "[The wrong of human sin] is extinguished. It is present only as something which has been eternally removed and destroyed" (IV/1, 553). Sin's removal occurs not only as the Son bears it away but also as he takes it into his divine life to destroy it.

Along with sin, death is destroyed at the same time insofar as death is sin's penalty and consequence. Christ trampled out death by death. "He . . . suffered eternal death on the cross . . . [and] by suffering it was destined to overcome it" (II/1, 404). Death's destruction occurred as he disempowered it from within (IV/1, 185). "He suffered death, and . . . robbed it of its power" (II/1, 626). God has overcome death through the death of his Son. "In taking our death to himself [on the cross] . . . God has conquered death and destroyed it" (IV/1, 481, rev.). God elected his only-begotten Son for this purpose. "By these events God confirms the fact that the Elect is the only-begotten Son of God who can suffer death but not be held by it, who by his death must destroy death" (II/2, 125, rev.). Death is removed as God submits to it, taking it into his own life to destroy it. "Mortality [is] swallowed up by life . . . and death in victory" (IV/1, 330). "He conquers by suffering" (IV/1, 238).

God remains superior to death even as he suffers it. In the mystery of the incarnation, he becomes human without ceasing to be God. He becomes temporal without ceasing to be eternal. He partakes of suffering without ceasing to be impassible. He submits to death while remaining in eternal life. All this is the high mystery of the incarnation.

It would be wrong to suppose that Barth denies God's impassibility. What he denies is that God's impassibility is an impediment to his sovereign freedom. He denies that God is a prisoner of his own perfections (IV/1, 187). Divine impassibility does not exist "above and behind [God's] living activity within the universe" (II/2, 79). On the contrary, it exists in and with that living activity as something present and operative even though concealed. In the cross of Christ, divine impassibility is hidden under the form of its opposite without ceasing to be what it is. Its concealment does not detract from its reality. "We know him even in this concealment. . . . He has acted as the true Son of God even in his suffering of death on the cross" (IV/2, 350). "When he goes into the far country," he "conceals his glory. . . . This concealment . . . is the image and reflection in which we see him as he is" (IV/1, 188).

It is beyond question that for Barth "God . . . is transcendent, free, sovereign, above the world, and therefore above the limitation and suffering of the human situation" (IV/1, 134). This ongoing transcendence reflects "the wealth of his perfections and his own inner life" (IV/1, 66). What Barth denies is that God ceases to be all these things "when he makes it his glory to be in the depths" (IV/1, 134). "God is always God even in his humiliation" (IV/1, 179). "He humbled himself, but he did not do it by ceasing to be who he is" (IV/1, 180). He did not cease to be "absolute, infinite, exalted, active, impassible, transcendent" (IV/1, 187). "He is all this as the Lord, and in such a way that he embraces the opposites of these concepts even while he is superior to them" (IV/1, 187). "He could have remained satisfied with himself and with the impassible glory and blessedness of his own inner life. But he did not do so" (II/2, 166). He is "the Most High who humbles himself and in that way is exalted and very high" (IV/1, 192).

> God gives himself, but he does not give himself away. He does not give up being God in becoming a creature, in becoming human. He does not cease to be God. He does not come into conflict with himself. He does not sin when in unity with the man Jesus he mingles with sinners and takes their place. And when he dies in his unity with this man, death does not gain any power over him. (IV/1, 185, rev.)

> He can be God and act as God in an absolute way and also a relative, in an infinite and also a finite, in an exalted and also a lowly, in an active and also a passive, in a transcendent and also an immanent, and finally, in a divine and also a human [way]. (IV/1, 187)

> [Divine freedom is] the freedom in which God can be lowly as well as exalted, abroad as well as at home, our God in the hidden form of One who is accused and judged as well as in himself (and known only to himself) the Lord of glory. (IV/1, 194)

> In virtue of this omnipotence, God's mercy could be at one and the same time the deepest and sincerest pity and inflexible and impassible divine strength. He could yield to his own inexorable righteousness and by this very surrender maintain himself as God. He could reveal himself at once as the One who as the servant of all bore the punishment of death which we had deserved, and the One who as the Lord of all took from death its power and for ever vanquished and destroyed it. (II/1, 400)

In Jesus Christ God is the Lord in the form of a servant, and as a servant he remains the Lord. In allowing himself to be humiliated and dishonored for the sake of the world, "he has not renounced and lost himself as God . . . he has not abdicated from his deity" (IV/1, 246). The Lord of all life shows that in some unfathomable way "he can really die and be dead" (IV/1, 246). "In this humiliation God is supremely God, . . . in this death he is supremely alive, . . . he has maintained and revealed his deity in the passion of this man as his eternal Son" (IV/1, 246–47). Without the elements of sovereignty and transcendence, God could not have triumphed over sin and death. Nevertheless, how God can be "supremely alive" in death surpasses all human understanding. What Barth says in a slightly different vein would also apply here. In this event what transpires is "not at all self-evident, but inconceivable in itself" (IV/2, 109). "Because it has the character of miracle, the knowledge of it will include an acknowledgment of the inexplicable and inconceivable nature of its occurrence" (IV/2, 149).

Barth's use of paradoxical language at this point is reminiscent of ancient Greek fathers, perhaps most especially Cyril of Alexandria.[10]

10. Barth himself cites Ignatius of Antioch ("the passion of God"), Irenaeus of Lyons ("the invisible was made visible, and the incomprehensible comprehensible,

Cyril, like Barth, resorted to paradox before the mystery of the cross. He too taught that the incarnate Son died without ceasing to be impassible and immortal. He famously or infamously suggested that the Son "suffered impassibly" and "died immortally."[11] In a way that would remain definitive for the church through the centuries, Cyril stated, "The manner of the union is entirely beyond human understanding."[12]

However, Barth may have been closer to Gregory of Nazianzus at this point than he was even to Cyril. According to Christopher A. Beeley, Gregory did not hesitate to develop the significance of the cross in theopaschite terms. The unity of Christ meant that God suffered not only in his human nature but also in his deity. In him it was God himself who suffered and died for our sake. Christ was "God made passible for our sake against sin" so that we were "saved by the sufferings of the impassible one" (*Or.* 30.1, 5). In him God underwent the full depth of human (creaturely) suffering and death in his own being. His divine nature destroyed our sin and death as fire melts wax. The passion of Christ was an "impassible passion" in which God was crucified without ceasing to be God.[13]

What Barth shared with Gregory was a single-subject Christology. The unity of Christ meant that the sufferings God endured in his humanity did not remain restricted to that plane. Through his human nature they were mediated to his divine nature by which they were eternally destroyed. Whereas Gregory spoke of fire at this point as melting wax, Barth spoke of it as consuming dry wood. Although Cyril of Alexandria seemed to vacillate about whether God could suffer in his divine nature,[14] Gregory and Barth did not. For both, the transcendent element in Christ's sufferings and death was the consuming fire of the divine life. The mystery of the divine nature in Christ was

---

and the impassible passible"), and Melito of Sardis ("the impassible suffers, and does not take revenge; the immortal dies and says no word in reply") (IV/1, 176–77, citations translated).

11. See Cyril of Alexandria, "Letter 4" (Second Letter to Nestorius), sec. 5, in *Letters 1–50* (Washington, DC: Catholic University of America Press, 1987), 40; "Letter 17" (Third Letter to Nestorius), anath. 12, in *Letters 1–50*, 92.

12. Quoted by G. L. Prestige, *Fathers and Heretics* (London: SPCK, 1940), 169.

13. See Christopher A. Beeley, *The Unity of Christ: Continuity and Conflict in the Patristic Tradition* (New Haven: Yale University Press, 2012), 192–93, 266–67.

14. Ibid., 269–70.

such that it became passible without ceasing to be impassible—and through impassibility prevailed.[15]

In short, Barth interpreted the sufferings and death of Christ according to the mystery of the Chalcedonian pattern. It was a pattern of asymmetrical unity-in-distinction. The inseparable unity meant that Christ's sufferings and death took place in his humanity without being strictly confined there. Through the flesh of the Word made flesh, they were mediated into the being of God, where they were destroyed as through a raging fire. Moreover, Christ's sufferings and death at the human level remained abidingly distinct from what God experienced at the divine level. The human sufferings were human, and the divine sufferings were divine—sufferings of the Father as well as of the Son—even as the two were one, "distinguishable in logic but inseparable in fact" (IV/2, 56). It was, however, the asymmetrical element that was decisive. If God had not remained impassible in his sufferings and eternally alive in his death, neither sin nor death would have been destroyed (II/1, 400). How God could really have suffered and died on the cross without ceasing to be truly God is the surpassing mystery of the incarnation.

Professor Jones's Argument Revisited

When Professor Jones writes about God's "self-determination" (as opposed to his ontological self-transformation), he is on stronger ground. Here are examples of some of his more modest but still important claims. "God's self-determination is grounded in, and particularized by, the realization of God's elective will in the person of Jesus Christ. The humanity of God is therefore derivative of God's loving self-determination, as Son, to become incarnate in Jesus Christ" (79).[16] "God has determined [himself] as Son in terms of an ontologically and agentially complex person, the existence of whom has an irreducibly contingent historical reference" (256). "One can even say that, given the Son's self-determination, God himself undergoes,

15. As also in Barth, impassibility was an important indicator of God's sovereign freedom for a number of patristic authors, such as Augustine and Cyril.

16. Citations in the text from Jones, *Humanity of Christ*.

prayerfully, what Jesus undergoes, prayerfully, in Gethsemane" (237). "Since God self-determines as Christ, there is no absolute event of diremption within the divine life" when Jesus cries out in dereliction from the cross (228). When he speaks in this register, I believe Professor Jones is correct.

What he does not seem to grasp, however, is that for Barth God can indeed determine himself without ontologically transforming himself. He fails to see that Barth develops his doctrine of antecedence and his post-Anselmian definitions of the divine perfections precisely to ensure that God can determine himself for humiliation, suffering, and death without undergoing ontological transformation. Professor Jones thinks that God historicizes his eternal being, but that would be precisely the kind of "admixture" (*Vermischung*) or "transformation" (*Veranderung*) that Barth explicitly rules out.

Barth argues instead that God can add the form of a servant to himself without losing the form of God, without ceasing to be the Lord, without failing to be Wholly Other, and without erasing the "infinite qualitative difference" between creaturely and divine being or the ontological divide between time and eternity. The "history" or dynamism inherent in the triune God ($history_1$) would be there whether the world were created or not because it is not a contingent but a noncontingent property. Professor Jones is correct, however, that God's decision to become incarnate in pretemporal election affects God's concrete identity materially and radically, especially because it leads God himself to suffer and die for us in Christ on the cross. Professor Jones's book spurs us to see this point with renewed clarity. Like other Barth-revisionists, however, he fails to grasp how many wheels within wheels Barth's dialectical engine can keep spinning.[17]

17. I owe this image to Robert W. Jenson. See his "Response" in *Union Seminary Quarterly Review* 28 (1972): 31–34; on 31.

Conclusion

In conclusion, it may be useful to draw together some of our positive findings. These pertain mainly to (1) the persistence of the Logos *asarkos*, (2) the Trinity as the presupposition of election, (3) Jesus Christ as the Subject of election, (4) the Son's eternal history of obedience to the Father as the antecedent ground of his obedience in the economy, (5) the coexistence of Anselmian and Hegelian elements in Barth's actualism, (6) divine immutability in election and incarnation, and finally (7) the suffering of the impassible God. These are all points that have become controversial in light of Barth-revisionism. A careful reading of Barth has shown that revisionist arguments on these matters cannot be sustained.

1. The Persistence of the Logos *Asarkos*

Although Barth strongly criticized the doctrine of the Logos *asarkos*, he did not reject it completely. His rejection pertained more to the knowledge of God than to the doctrine of God. He was adamant that the Logos *asarkos* had no role to play in our coming to know God. Allotting it such a role would be tantamount to natural theology, which Barth of course famously opposed. Knowledge of God was strictly a matter of revealed theology through the history of the covenant as fulfilled in the Word made flesh. Only through the mediation of enfleshed Word, not through the Logos *asarkos*, were we granted a share in God's own self-knowledge as Father, Son, and Holy Spirit. The only form of the divine Word to which we had access was the incarnate Word, Jesus Christ.

Nevertheless, in line with historic Reformed theology, Barth continued to affirm the so-called *extra Calvinisticum* and with it a role for the Logos *asarkos* within God's inner life. In the incarnation, the Word of God was totally but not exhaustively present. There was more to the eternal God's self-relationship than just his world-relationship. In and with his relationship to the world, God maintained at the same time a relationship in and for himself, which in certain respects was accessible only to himself. However, whether in and for himself or in and for the world, God was never any other than the triune God who loves in freedom. God's revelation of his triune identity in the economy corresponded fully to his triune identity in himself to all eternity.

This line of interpretation helps us to see how Barth could reject the Logos *asarkos* so forcefully in one mood while quietly affirming it in another. For the doctrine of God, he could still presuppose, to borrow words from another context, that the Logos *asarkos* is "real in God in a form which is concealed from us and incomprehensible to us" (II/1, 357). He could embrace the Logos *asarkos* as "the second mode of existence ('person') of the *inner* divine reality *in itself* and *as such*" (III/1, 50, original italics restored). He could regard the Logos *asarkos* as "the Word in which God speaks with himself, thinks himself, and is conscious of himself" to all eternity (III/2, 147). He could contend, to the surprise of many, that "in himself and as such [the eternal Logos] is not revealed to us. In himself and as such he is not *Deus pro nobis*, either ontologically or epistemologically" (IV/1, 52). He could point to the theological necessity of such an idea: "It is true that it [the Logos *asarkos*] has shown itself necessary to the christological and trinitarian reflections of the Church. Even today it is indispensable for dogmatic enquiry and presentation" (III/1, 54). He could explain this necessity as a matter of upholding the freedom of God. "He [the Logos *asarkos*] is the content of a necessary and important concept in trinitarian doctrine when we have to understand the revelation and dealings of God in the light of their free basis in the inner being and essence of God" (IV/1, 52). The Logos *asarkos* was regarded as primordial in the Trinity and perpetual as the free basis of the incarnation.

2. The Trinity as the Presupposition of Election

Once revisionism's deductive reasoning is placed to one side, there is no reason not to affirm the direct wording of Barth's texts.

> The Subject of this decision is the triune God—the Son of God no less than the Father and the Holy Spirit. (II/2, 110)

> The Son of God determined to give himself from all eternity. With the Father and the Holy Spirit, he chose to unite himself with the lost Son of Man. This Son of Man was from all eternity the object of the election of Father, Son, and Holy Spirit. (II/2, 158)

> In the inner life of God—as the eternal essence of Father, Son, and Holy Ghost—the divine essence does not, of course, need any actualization. On the contrary, it is the creative ground of all other, i.e., all creaturely actualizations. Even as the divine essence of the Son, it did not need his incarnation, his existence as man . . . to become actual. (IV/2, 113, rev.)

> [The triune] God does not, therefore, become the living God when he works or decides to work *ad extra*—in his being *ad extra* he is, of course, the living God in a different way—but his being and activity *ad extra* is merely an overflowing of his inward activity and being. (II/2, 175, rev.)

The Holy Trinity, for Barth, has no beginning because the Holy Trinity is God, and God by definition has no beginning. There is nothing in Barth to suggest that the Trinity is subsequent to election. As he states repeatedly, God would be sufficient in himself as Father, Son, and Holy Spirit whether the world were created or not. "Nothing would be lacking in his inward being as God in glory—as the Father, Son, and Holy Spirit— . . . if he had refrained from giving [the world] being when he created it out of nothing" (IV/1, 213, rev.).

3. Jesus Christ as the Subject of Election

Revisionism is right to contend that Barth sees Jesus Christ as the Subject of election in his full divine-human unity. What it fails to see is that Barth posits this unity as present proleptically in pretemporal eternity. In and through the decision of the eternal Son, Jesus himself is present as "the man who was in the beginning with God." He is present as "the man who was marked and sought out by God's love." He is present as "the man to whom and to the existence of whom the whole work of God applied as it was predetermined from all eternity" (II/2, 180). "But as this creature—because this is what God sees and wills—he is before all things, *even before the dawn of his own time*" (IV/2, 33, rev.; italics added). "In this free act of the election of grace there is already present, and presumed, and assumed into unity with his own existence as God, the existence of the man whom he intends and loves from the very first" (IV/1, 66). "At no level or time can we have to do with God without having also to do with this man. . . . But as the one whom God has elected and willed, he was and is there first, . . . there in being" (IV/2, 33, rev.). Even before the dawn of his own time, he is present in eternity as the one he will be in the economy by virtue of the gracious divine counsel and foreknowledge. "He existed in the counsel of God from all eternity and before creation" (III/1, 51).

Pretemporal election is a complex transaction that unfolds as follows. The Father elects the Son; the Son elects himself in free obedience to the Father; in electing himself the Son also elects the human Jesus into unity with himself; the man Jesus elects himself by consenting to be the object of divine election; and finally the man Jesus consents to his election by electing the God who elected him. Remarkably, all this is seen as occurring in pretemporal eternity. In this pretemporal occurrence, the man Jesus is thought to be present with the Holy Trinity in a unique way, namely, from before the foundation of the world. He is present proleptically according to the eternal counsel and foreknowledge of God.

Jesus Christ is thus the Subject of pretemporal election in the unity of his divine and human willing. "He is not, of course, a second God. He is not eternal as God is. He is only the creature of God—bound to time, limited in other ways too. . . . But as this creature—because this is what God sees and wills—he is before all things" (IV/2, 33, rev.). Precisely as this timebound creature, and in unity with the Son, the human Jesus takes part proleptically in the pretemporal decision of election.

4. The Son's Eternal History of Obedience to the Father

In discussing "the obedience of the Son" in IV/1, Barth uses the term *history* in a way that is potentially misleading. It does not refer merely to the Son's obedience in the economy (history_2) but refers primarily to his antecedent obedience in eternity (history_1). These two different histories are radically and abidingly distinct. Although the economic form is the outward unfolding of the eternal form, they are related asymmetrically—and therefore irreversibly and irreducibly. As is typical in Barth, the eternal form serves as the antecedent basis of the economic form. The Son's eternal history of obedience to the Father would be what it is regardless of whether the Son had elected to become incarnate. The two histories are related by grace, not by nature—by a pattern of asymmetrical unity-in-distinction, not by a pattern of dialectical identity. They are not two correlative forms of a single history, the one eternal and the other economic. On the contrary, they are instead two radically distinct histories united in Christ through the mystery of the hypostatic union, in which the eternal form is noncontingent while the economic form is contingent.

In the mystery of the hypostatic union, God adds to himself what did not previously belong to him. The event of the incarnation is new even for God. "He becomes what he had not previously been. He takes into unity with his divine being a quite different, a creaturely and indeed a sinful being. . . . But . . . he does not do it apart from its basis in his own being, in his own inner life" (IV/1, 203). He does it in "correspondence [*Entsprechung*] to . . . the [eternal] history in which he is God." Therefore, what God does in the economy can be described as the "miraculously consistent ultimate continuation" (*wunderbar konsequente letzte Fortsetzung*) of "the history in which he is God" (IV/1, 203, rev.). Revisionism misreads this passage—and the entire context in which it occurs—as if Barth were working with a correlative pattern of "dialectical identity" as opposed to his usual pattern of an asymmetrical "unity-in-distinction." It misreads him, in other words, as if he were operating with a more or less "Hegelian" ontology as opposed to the "Chalcedonian" pattern. It overlooks that Barth continues to uphold "an absolute (and infinitely qualitative) distinction" between divine and human being (IV/2, 61). It fails to see that God's being remains "Wholly Other" (*qualitativ Andere*) in eternity (IV/1, 176). Barth's use of the term *history* here does not efface but presupposes the ontological divide between the Creator and the creature.

5. The Coexistence of Anselmian and Hegelian Elements

Despite (or because of) his strong actualistic tendencies, Barth continued to uphold in some form an "Anselmian" or perfect-being theology. He continued to affirm that God's being was entirely self-existent and self-sufficient, lacking nothing in and for itself. He continued to presuppose in some form God's aseity (IV/3, 80), simplicity (III/2, 218), immutability (IV/1, 561), impassibility (IV/1, 187), and eternality (II/2, 19). The question was not whether these predicates belonged to God but rather in what sense they did so. They had to be recast (but not discarded) in a way that differed from classical theism.

Most especially, these essential properties had to be defined so that they were compatible with the sovereign freedom of the living God. They could not be posited abstractly, as if each were some sort of inert and inflexible absolute. Otherwise they would make it impossible for God to enter into the world without contradicting his divine essence. They had to be conceived as the antecedent basis of all God's ways and works with the world. They were not the inhibition of those works, nor were they a subsequent result of them. God did not need to transform himself in order to be God for us in Jesus Christ. Whatever God did in the economy had its antecedent ground in eternity. His perfections and eternal predications had to be thought through accordingly.

God could have remained satisfied with "the wealth of his perfections" (IV/1, 66). His inner life lacks nothing in itself (II/2, 121). He exists in a "perfection . . . which needs no filling" (IV/1, 201). "This God is self-sufficient. [He] knows perfect beatitude in himself" (IV/2, 346). Barth's emphasis on divine perfection represents the Anselmian moment in his theology.

The Hegelian elements are tempered by the Anselmian elements.[1] An example may be seen in Barth's doctrine of the incarnation. Barth realized that taken by itself, the Chalcedonian definition might give the impression that the incarnation was something static and immobile (IV/1, 127). Like any grammar, it did not stand on its own but needed to be fleshed out. Barth did that in an "actualistic" way. As he explained, "We have 'actualized' the doctrine of the incarnation, i.e., we have used the main traditional concepts . . . as . . . terms to describe one and the same ongoing process. We have stated it all (including the Chalcedonian definition, which is so important in dogmatic history, and rightly became normative) in the form of a . . . description of a single event" (IV/2, 105). This way of actualizing the incarnation represents Barth's "Hegelian" moment.

At the same time, it is noteworthy that Barth also stressed the incarnation as a "completed fact" (IV/2, 45). As God's eternal will accomplished in time, the incarnation had to be described as "a once-for-all perfect event" (IV/2, 45, rev.). It would thus qualify, in Barth's terms, as a "perfect work" (*opus perfectus*) (I/1, 427). However, Barth did not stop at this point. He went on to introduce a dialectical counterpart. He conceived of this perfect work, dialectically, as also involving an ongoing history. "It is equally important to remember that this [completed] fact is an event. The act of God in which it is a fact—and without which it would not be—is *completed*; but it is completed in its occurrence as the *act of God*. The incarnation thus represents a being which as such does not cease to be a becoming: *et homo factus est* [and he was *made* man]" (IV/2, 46, rev.).

Just as God's own being is in becoming, so the perfection of the incarnation also includes an aspect of becoming—an *actus perpetuus* (I/1, 427). The perfect work would not be perfect—and would not be divine—without this second element of perpetual operation. God's

1. By the same token, we could say that the Anselmian elements are vivified by the Hegelian elements.

own unique becoming does not involve a transition from potentiality to actuality. His becoming is rather a living and perfect becoming, continually actualizing itself for what it is. It does so ever anew. It is a continual re-actualization of itself in its inherent perfection. God's becoming is a living movement from actuality to actuality and from perfection to perfection.

What Barth says about God's becoming is also applied to the incarnation. "To celebrate Christmas," he wrote, "is to think of the *perfectum* [perfect occurrence] but with a remembrance—and indeed in the truth and presence—of the *perficere* [perfecting] in which alone it is always actuality" (IV/2, 46, rev.). The perfect reality of the incarnation (*perfectum*) is not actual except in an ongoing event of "perfecting" (*perficere*), that is, of re-actualizing itself in its perfection again and again.

Anchored in time as a once-for-all event, the incarnation also transcends time. It is an "act of that becoming which—as the Son of God once became human in time—can never become past or cease to be his act" (IV/2, 46, rev.). In a similar vein, Barth could write,

> We have in fact to do with his act. And first, this means generally—with an event, with a happening. But as such this is an event which is in no sense to be transcended. It is not, therefore, an event which has merely happened and is now a past fact of history. [It] is, of course, this as well. But it is also an event happening in the present, here and now. (II/1, 262, rev.)

The idea of the incarnation as a once-for-all historical event that nonetheless transcends time by pervading it and making itself present through a perpetual operation represents Barth's unique way of thinking about Christology. The incarnation is always an *opus perfectus* and yet also an *actus perpetuus*.

These two ideas, taken in combination, represent the essence of Barth's actualism. The former idea, I suggest, owes something to Anselm (*opus perfectus*), while the latter owes something to Hegel (*actus perpetuus*). Despite revisionist tendencies to accentuate the perpetual aspect while neglecting the completed and perfect aspect, neither operated in Barth without the other. Furthermore, despite efforts to regard Barth's actualism as an ontology, it is much more nearly a *Denkform*, or a dialectical mode of thought. It is a motif he uses to describe the utter singularity of divine events like the incarnation.[2]

6. Divine Immutability in Election and Incarnation

In Barth a doctrine of divine antecedence took precedence over all elements of subsequence. He argued that the Lord God remained the same in and through every change. What remained the same were his eternal constituents and his essential predications. They remained constant in and through the adding of every new differentia. Indeed, God's eternal constituents and essential predications were the basis of his freedom to add new differentiae to himself without losing himself. His freedom presupposed these constancies.

Stated less formally, God's eternal constituents were the terms of his triune identity; his essential predications were properties like aseity, simplicity, eternality, and impassibility, and the adding of new differentiae was what Barth meant by self-determination. God determined himself through election and incarnation—he added new differentiae to himself—without thereby constituting his triune identity or transforming his essential properties. That God could determine himself without retooling himself was the essence of Barth's doctrine of immutability.

For Barth, God did not need to become ontologically other in order to become incarnate in Jesus Christ. He did not need to constitute himself as the Trinity, nor did he need to "historicize" his eternal being. He could become the Trinity in the economy because he was already the Trinity to all eternity. Likewise, in his trinitarian mode as the Son, he could become obedient in earthly history because he was already obedient in the eternal history inherent within the immanent Trinity. Neither his trinitarian identity nor his essential historicity were subsequent to election and the incarnation. On the contrary, his

2. For an elaboration and application of Barth's actualism, see the charts in my book *The Eucharist and Ecumenism: Let Us Keep the Feast* (Cambridge: Cambridge University Press, 2008), 184–85.

identity as the eternal Trinity was antecedent to its manifestation in the economy. Similarly, his eternal historicity was antecedent to his economic historicity.

Any subsequence in God was dependent on these forms of pure antecedence. Any secondary divine contingencies were dependent on his primary (and absolute) noncontingency. Any new differentiae that God added to himself in election and the incarnation presupposed the constancy of his triune identity, essential properties, and eternal historicity. His antecedent identity, properties, and historicity were in fact the free basis of his incarnation, while his incarnation presupposed the constancy of these characteristics in his divine being. Although the incarnation made a real material difference for God, it did not make a difference in his primordial identity. Divine immutability, for Barth, was not only ethical but also ontological.[3]

7. The Suffering of the Impassible God

Divine impassibility is perhaps the test case for this interpretation of how Barth viewed God's constancy or immutability. Could God, as Barth taught, eternally destroy suffering and death by taking them into his own being without ceasing to be God? Could God remain God beyond all suffering and death while still making them his own in Jesus Christ? Could he partake of the cross while remaining immutable and impassible? Could he really suffer while transcending his suffering? Could he really die while retaining himself in eternal life? Could he maintain his perfect being in dying for our sins in Christ?

Barth believed that God could not be affected by anything other than himself. Therefore, nothing external to God could possibly subject him to suffering and death. If God underwent these afflictions, it could only be by an act of sovereign freedom. Sovereign freedom was what made it possible for God to assume suffering and death into himself while at the same time destroying them eternally as he did so.

Sovereign freedom is God's freedom as the Lord. God is the Lord not only over all suffering and death but also over his own essential

3. This is a point of great divergence between the traditionalists and the revisionists.

predicates. As Luther had stressed, God is free to take the form of his opposite on the cross without ceasing to be Lord over all that assailed him. For Barth, God is even the Lord, not the prisoner, of his own impassibility. His impassibility does not prevent him from deliberately entering into suffering and death. It is rather the transcendent element that allows him to triumph over suffering and death even as he assumes them into himself. God remains impassible in sovereign transcendence even as he makes himself passible in his assumption of the flesh. The weakness of God is stronger than the wood of the cross (cf. 1 Cor. 1:25).

No nonparadoxical formulation can capture the mystery of this occurrence. Reminiscent of Cyril and Gregory, Barth therefore wrote, "In this humiliation God is supremely God, . . . in this death he is supremely alive, . . . he has maintained and revealed his deity in the passion of this man as his eternal Son" (IV/1, 246–47). For Barth, God is never more truly God than in the freedom of his self-humiliation, never more basically impassible than when he overcomes suffering by his wounds, and never more fully alive than when he tramples out death by death. God's perfect being is not only maintained but also made manifest in his destruction of sin and death on the cross. In his suffering and death, the impassible God remains powerfully transcendent and strong to save.

Final Thoughts

1. The Question of a Single-Act Perspective

Barth-revisionism has argued that the Trinity is not fully constituted apart from election. Election must be seen as constitutive of God's trinitarian being at least in part (so the argument goes) because election and the Trinity both belong to the same eternal divine act. Revisionism has vigorously rejected the idea of regarding God's eternal activity as if it were a "two-act drama." It rightly contends that, at least from one standpoint, God's eternal activity requires a "single act" perspective. For Barth, the one *actus purus et singularis* in which God has his being is also the act in which he elects Jesus Christ, through whom he creates the world.

What revisionism fails to see, however, is that for Barth this single act is internally differentiated and complex. For Barth, the single-act perspective does not mean that the distinction between the contingent and the noncontingent is nullified. Nor does it mean that the triune God's activity *ad extra* is constitutive in any sense of his eternal being. Nor again does it mean that just because God's relationship to the world has a "beginning," God's own constitution as the Trinity must also have a beginning.

As we have seen, when Barth states that God has no beginning, he means that the Holy Trinity as such has no beginning. The single-act perspective must therefore be conceived in such a way that it allows for a contingent aspect and a noncontingent aspect. Barth distinguishes, for example, between God's "absolute being" and his "contingent will" (*von absolutem Sein und kontingentem Willen Gottes*) (III/1, 15). God's absolute being is his eternal reality as the Trinity, while his contingent will pertains to election and creation. As previously noted, Barth often gestures toward such a distinction by using the word *also*. The single act in which God enjoys his absolute being also includes his contingent will by which he relates to the world.

Election and creation thus take place, for Barth, "by the [contingent] will and act of God" (III/1, 14). "There was no other necessity than that of his own free love" (III/1, 51). God's absolute being is already a perfect being in and for itself. As Barth never tires of repeating, the triune God "could have remained satisfied with the fullness of his own being. If he had willed and decided to remain so, he would not have suffered any lack. He would still be eternal love and freedom" (III/1, 69, rev.). "Of course he did not need [creation's] completion to be God, to be glorious in himself, to be blessed and free and joyful. But the very fact that he does not keep this inner glory to himself is the demonstration of his grace in the creation of this world" (III/1, 223). The single act in which God enjoys his perfect being as the Trinity does not prevent him from also having a contingent will with respect to election and creation.

The point is that nothing in the very idea of "a single divine act" prevents God from possessing both absolute being and a contingent will. Here Barth clearly resembles "classical theists" like Aquinas. Aquinas also affirmed that God's triune being was pure act, was perfect and sufficient in itself, and did not exclude a contingent divine will. Barth clearly aligned himself with the medieval Dominican in this regard. He noted that Aquinas upheld "the most important statement in the doctrine of creation—namely, that of the *novitas mundi* [contingency of the world]" (III/1, 4, rev.). Barth also endorsed Aquinas's teaching "that the world is not eternal but has a beginning." He agreed with him that the idea of creation's contingency "is only *credibile, non autem scibile et demonstrabile* [a matter of belief, not of immediate knowledge or rational demonstration] (*S. theol.*, I, *qu.* 46, *art.* 2*c*)" (III/1, 4).

As in Aquinas so also in Barth, the idea of the world's contingency—as grounded in God's contingent will—was not derived from reason but from revelation. It was a matter of evangelical reasoning, not rational demonstration. In short, there is no good reason why affirming God's contingent will in election and creation should logically commit one to a "two-act drama" in eternity.

This is not the same as saying, however, that a single-act perspective is the only possible one. For the sake of convenience it is also permissible to speak not only of election as a free contingent (unnecessary) decision but also of creation as a new divine act—over against the primordial (non-contingent) divine act in which God posits himself absolutely as the Trinity (I/1, 435).[4]

2. God as Unconditioned by Anything Other Than Himself

Before closing, I want to revisit Professor van Driel's line of reasoning about how revisionism is related to Hegel. Professor van Driel had observed that incarnation presupposes creation; therefore, "if election is essential to God, then so is creation." It would follow that "creation is constitutive of divine being." Revisionism would to that extent land in the same place as Hegel, "even if [its] starting point—will rather than nature—is different."[5] In other words, like Hegel, revisionism makes the creation necessary to God's essential being insofar as the triune God cannot constitute himself without it (or something like it).

4. Revisionism is overly strict in not allowing for this looser way of speaking.

5. Edwin van Driel, "Karl Barth on the Eternal Existence of Jesus Christ," *Scottish Journal of Theology* 60 (2007): 45–61; on 54. References hereafter are in the text.

In rebuttal, Professor McCormack made three points.[6]

- First, in contrast to revisionism, "Hegel works consistently from the general . . . to the particular" (69). He "makes Jesus to be the revelation of something that is true of all human beings" (69). Accordingly, for Hegel, the universal "is made explicit" in Jesus (69).
- Second, for revisionism (in contrast to Hegel), "what is 'essential' to God is only what takes place in Jesus himself and not what takes place in us" (70).
- Finally, for Hegel (in contrast to revisionism), "the ontological distinction between God and humankind is set aside" (70). Revisionism, on the other hand, follows Barth in making God's relation to human beings a function of his relation to Jesus, a relation in which the ontological distinction between God and the world is upheld.

What are we to make of these rebuttals? While they certainly differentiate revisionism from Hegel, the main thing to see is that they fail to address Professor van Driel's concern: that if election is essential to God, creation is also. The first is beside the point since it pertains not to God's trinitarian self-constitution but to how anthropology is related to Christology. The third again changes the subject because it pertains not to God's self-constitution but to the ontological difference between God and the world. By the way, it is noteworthy that revisionism, with its more recent polemic against an "ontological gap," has increasingly tended toward panentheism, in which the "ontological distinction" between God and the world is eroded and relativized. Finally, the second rebuttal is extraordinary because it virtually concedes Professor van Driel's point. If what is "essential" to God is what takes place in the human Jesus, then it clearly depends on an aspect of the created world.

Professor van Driel had asked about the scandal of somehow making God's essential being dependent on the world. To that extent God

6. Bruce McCormack, "Seek God Where He May Be Found: A Response to Edwin Chr. van Driel," *Scottish Journal of Theology* 60 (2007): 62–79. References hereafter are in the text.

would be conditioned by the world since God could not be God (or the Trinity) without it. What we have here is the unfortunate consequence of forcing Barth into the mold of an "actualistic ontology." For Barth, nothing is necessary for the triune God to be what he is other than himself (aseity). In particular, God's triune being cannot be understood as needing to be constituted through his relation to creation. God would be robbed of his freedom to the extent that he depended upon the creation to constitute himself, even as creation would be robbed of its gratuity insofar as it was necessary to God's constituting his triune identity.

> God would be no less God if he had created no world and no human being. The existence of the world and our own existence are in no sense vital to God, not even as the object of his love. The eternal generation of the Son by the Father tells us first and supremely that God is not at all lonely even without the world and us. His love has its object in himself. (I/1, 139–40, rev.)

> The right understanding of the freedom of God's will excludes all those views which seek to represent the relation between God and the reality distinct from himself as a relation of mutual limitation and necessity. In the first instance this includes all pantheistic and panentheistic systems, according to which the existence of this other reality belongs in some way to the essence and existence of God himself. The reason why God gives them real being . . . is not that God would not be God without their actual or even possible existence. . . . As real objects of his will . . . they are distinct from him. He is not conditioned by them. . . . He has called them and created them out of nothing. He was not obliged to do this. He did not do it to satisfy some need in his own being and life. . . . He is always free in relation to these objects. (II/1, 562, rev.)

> What God did in Jesus Christ—what the Son of God present and active in him did—was to unite in himself two who could not be brought together in any other way—God with man and man with God—not on any other ground, or in any other power, or caused and conditioned in any other way, but *per seipsum* [through himself]. God in Jesus Christ founded and created this "also," his being as the One who is both very God and very man. (IV/2, 41, rev.)

Barth insists that God's being is unconditioned. His perfect-being theology, as I interpret it, logically requires the Logos *asarkos* insofar as it safeguards against trying to make God's being somehow dependent on the world. The Logos *asarkos* belongs to God's perfect, absolute, and all-sufficient being, which lacks nothing in itself. God's being as the Trinity does not need the world (not even the human Jesus) in order to be what it is.

It is therefore no wonder that revisionism wishes to eliminate the Logos *asarkos* from Barth's theology because otherwise it could not claim Barth as its precedent. The Logos *asarkos* blocks revisionism from claiming Barth for its project of transforming the triune God's absolute being into something essentially conditioned and contingent. It blocks it from discarding Barth's Anselmian elements while keeping only those that are Hegelian.[7]

As Professor van Driel points out, revisionism also attempts to differentiate itself from Hegel on the question of the trinitarian processions. For Hegel the processions are said to be "natural," whereas for revisionism they are "willed by God." According to revisionism, a Hegelian approach would be one for which the act of divine self-differentiation is "necessary" as opposed to being "a free act." For Hegel, creation and reconciliation thereby become necessary as well (53).

It would seem that there are several revisionist confusions here. Most important, revisionism attempts to make the processions belong to God's contingent will rather than to his absolute being, which is diametrically opposed to Barth. At the same time, revisionism blurs two different senses of the word *necessity*. For Hegel, the processions are metaphysically necessary in the sense that God needs them in order to constitute himself through the history of the world. For Barth they are necessary in the sense that they belong to the triune God's absolute being in eternity by definition. For revisionism they belong to God essentially by virtue of his contingent will in relation to the world.

Barth therefore differs from both Hegel and revisionism in that for him the trinitarian processions are constituted antecedently to election and creation. By contrast, for both Hegel and revisionism,

7. The Logos *asarkos*, of course, is not the only moment in Barth that blocks any effort at a Hegelian reduction. In this regard it is simply representative, not exclusive.

the processions are somehow subsequent to God's relation to the world. The doctrine of subsequence is what unites the revisionists with Hegel and separates them from Barth.

The doctrine of antecedence, on the other hand, is what unites Barth with a "classical theist" like Aquinas, who wrote in a way that Barth, whether early or late, could only endorse. "The mystery of the Incarnation [the visible mission of the Son] was not completed through God being changed in any way from the state in which he had been from eternity, but through his having united himself to the creature in a new way, or rather through having united it to himself" (*S. theol.*, III, qu. 1, art. 1, ad. 1).

For Barth as for Aquinas (in contrast to Hegel and the revisionists), the divine processions were antecedent to the divine missions in the same sense as eternity was prior to the economy. For Barth as for Aquinas, in other words, the Trinity was self-constituted and self-sufficient in and of itself to all eternity. In relation to election and creation, the triune constitution of God's being was for them never the consequence but always the prior ground.

Appendix

Analogia Entis in Balthasar and Barth

Great light has recently been cast by Junius Johnson on the Creator-creature relation as a technical question in Christian theology.[1] Although I think he does a better job with Hans Urs von Balthasar than with Karl Barth, Johnson gives us the analytical tools to bring these two theologians into focus more clearly than perhaps ever before. Drawing on Johnson's work, I want to explicate their views in terms of four theses.

1. Balthasar posits that pure difference and analogy are mutually exclusive. Barth, by contrast, develops a doctrine of analogy within the context of pure difference.
2. Balthasar accepts the formulation of the Fourth Lateran Council, whereas Barth rejects it.
3. Balthasar develops his doctrine of analogy by proposing a theological metaphysics. Barth expounds his doctrine of analogy by positing actualism as an alternative to metaphysics.

1. See his outstanding book *Christ and Analogy: The Christocentric Metaphysics of Hans Urs von Balthasar* (Minneapolis: Fortress, 2013).

4. The difference between Balthasar's metaphysics and Barth's actualism forms the crux of why they differ about the *analogia entis*.

Pure Difference and Analogy

According to Johnson, Balthasar outlines three ways for understanding the Creator-creature relation. One may say (a) that the Creator and creature are totally different, with absolutely nothing in common; (b) that they are totally the same, with no difference between them; or (c) that they are somehow metaphysically similar despite their radical differences. Johnson calls these views (a) the Pure Difference Thesis, (b) the Identity Thesis, and (c) the Analogy Thesis.

This way of setting up the problem already suggests why Barth and Balthasar had to diverge. For Balthasar, analogy and pure difference are mutually exclusive, whereas for Barth they are not.

The Fourth Lateran Council

As Johnson indicates, Balthasar subscribes to the formula decreed by the Fourth Lateran Council (1215): "A likeness is not able to be noted between the Creator and the creature unless a greater unlikeness is to be noted between them." This formula, which Balthasar often cites, gives classic expression to the analogy of being. He commonly abbreviates it as "similarity but always greater dissimilarity."

The "greater dissimilarity" was thought to be infinite in scope. It is important to note, however, that similarity and dissimilarity, despite their disparity, are conceived of as existing on a common scale. Balthasar can thus describe the Creator-creature relation as a matter of distance as well as of difference—that is, in terms that are quantitative as well as qualitative, even if the distance in question is infinite. He slides back and forth between these two terms.

For Balthasar, the similarity and the dissimilarity are thought to share a common measure and so are related by a certain proportionality according to which two realities, or two proportions, are similar despite belonging to radically different metaphysical types. On this account, the disjunction between God and the world is not absolute. The Fourth Lateran Council stands opposed (on this reading) to the idea of pure difference.[2]

Although Barth himself rejects the Lateran formula (I/1, 41), his reasons for doing so remain intuitive. He never explicitly explains what seems to him to be fairly obvious. In line with Barth, however, the basic intuition has been unpacked by Denys Turner.

> There can be no good sense . . . in any . . . calculation of the greater and lesser degrees of "distance" which lie between Creator and creatures as contrasted with that between one creature and another; for it is not on some common scale of difference that these differences differ . . . as if to say: it is this kind or that, only infinitely so. . . . A term of comparison . . . presupposes a common scale. . . . For if God is not any kind of being, then his difference from creatures is not a difference of any kind, hence is not a difference of any size, hence is not incomparably greater, but, on the contrary, is, simply, incommensurable. "Greater" and "lesser" cannot come into it, logically speaking.[3]

Turner continues,

> It is not, I said, *a* difference; it is such as to be "incommensurable"—that is to say, it is such that this difference cannot be set in *any* form of contrast with any sameness. For that reason, I have argued further, the difference between God and creatures cannot stand on the same logical ground that differences between creatures stand on.[4]

Although Turner would deal with this incommensurability in a different way than Barth, his argument highlights the logic inherent in the very idea of pure difference. It is a logic that Barth presupposes as well. Unlike Balthasar, Barth rejects the idea (fundamental to the *analogia entis*) that God and the creature are related by any kind of proportion or common scale. He would agree with Turner that

2. See ibid., 46, 60, 64, 95, 110, 142, 147, 161n46, etc.

3. Denys Turner, *Faith, Reason and the Existence of God* (Cambridge: Cambridge University Press, 2004), 213.

4. Ibid., 214.

since God is Wholly Other, God is not any kind of being. Contrary to Balthasar, for Barth the difference between God and the creature is incommensurable.

Metaphysics versus Actualism

Johnson helps us to see that Barth and Balthasar differ about the condition for the possibility of the incarnation. Balthasar finds it in a metaphysical scheme embracing the Creator and the creature, whereas Barth must look for it elsewhere. Balthasar assumes that a measure of ontological continuity is indispensable. Without similarity in the midst of greater dissimilarity, the incarnation would be neither possible nor intelligible. As Johnson explains, for Balthasar "no creature would be capable of bearing the divine person if there were no likeness between God and the creature."[5] The incarnation requires that there be a prior "created potency" in human nature.[6] "A likeness between Creator and creature is the necessary presupposition for Incarnation. Thus, if this likeness is denied, as it is in the Pure Difference Thesis, then Incarnation becomes logically impossible and Christology is destroyed."[7]

For Barth, by contrast, the incarnation must be seen as an absolute miracle (IV/2, 219). God is supremely free to become incarnate in Jesus Christ without ceasing to be God and also without doing violence to human nature. We cannot know on a priori grounds, Barth would say, that such an absolute miracle would be "unfitting," nor can we know that the incarnation would be "logically impossible" in the absence of a metaphysical likeness such as Balthasar posits.[8] For Barth, nothing exists in human nature to make it commensurable with the otherness of God and so with the high mystery of the incarnation. For him a priori arguments to the contrary are suppositious and must be rejected as unwarranted speculation.

For Barth, the incarnation finds the condition for its possibility entirely in God. It has no secondary ground in human nature, nor is it

5. Johnson, *Christ and Analogy*, 41.
6. Ibid.
7. Ibid., 58.
8. Ibid., 60.

"explicable in principle" from a metaphysical point of view (I/2, 181). On the contrary, it is purely a miracle. "The divine act of humility fulfilled in the Son is the only ground of this happening and being. On this ground the unity achieved in this history has to be described, not as two-sided, but as founded, and as consisting absolutely and exclusively, in him" (IV/2, 46–47 rev.). By the same token, "because it has the character of miracle, knowledge of [the incarnation] will include an acknowledgment of the inexplicable and inconceivable nature of its occurrence" (IV/2, 149 rev.).

In short, Balthasar's account of the incarnation is metaphysical where Barth's account is actualistic. Balthasar seeks a mode of "intelligibility" that Barth would regard as a category mistake. The incarnation, Barth argues, cannot be understood on any ground other than itself. Its intelligibility is a matter not of metaphysical explanation but instead of a miraculous history. Actualism would thus be Barth's alternative to Balthasar's metaphysics. From Barth's point of view, the degree of miracle that Balthasar himself posits for the incarnation, and the mode of intelligibility he affirms, on metaphysical grounds, cannot do justice to the absolute miracle of the incarnation and so to its surpassing mystery.

Analogia Entis

Balthasar insists that Barth's theology unwittingly entails an *analogia entis*. He did not see that Barth's actualism is an alternative to this idea. Balthasar argues that a metaphysical *analogia entis* is unavoidable, in part, because it is the necessary condition of the incarnation. Only such a metaphysical premise, he argues, could explain what made the incarnation possible and intelligible.

Barth's concept of pure difference means, however, that there can be no *analogia entis* presupposed by the incarnation. The incarnation was possible only as an absolute miracle and intelligible only as an incomprehensible mystery. God and the creature were (and remain) ontologically incommensurable in and with their indissoluble union in Christ. The ontological divide that exists by nature was mysteriously and miraculously overcome in the incarnation by an act of sovereign grace understood as a perfect work and a perpetual operation.

In short, with respect to the incarnation, what Balthasar ascribes by way of metaphysics to created nature, Barth posits instead as a particular history grounded uniquely in the sovereignty of God as operative in the miracle of grace.

Balthasar and Barth-Revisionism

Despite wide differences, it would seem that Balthasar and Barth-revisionism share at least one thing in common. Each proceeds in its own way to draw wide-ranging conclusions on the basis of deductive reasoning. Each argues that a metaphysics or an ontology is logically required to make the incarnation intelligible. For Balthasar it is a metaphysics of the *analogia entis*, whereas for Barth-revisionism it is an actualistic ontology (in the sense of $ontology_1$).

If the above analysis is correct, however, the whole point of Barth's actualism is to obviate any such metaphysical or ontological deductions. For Barth, there can be no *analogia entis*, because God and the creature are ontologically incommensurable. For the same reason, there can be no actualistic ontology that makes God's trinitarian identity dependent on the world. Actualism, in Barth's hands, was intended to uphold not only God's absolute otherness but also God's absolute aseity.

Author Index

Subject Index